OXFORD TEXTUAL PERSPECTIVES

The Visible Text

GENERAL EDITORS

Elaine Treharne   Greg Walker

The Visible Text

*Textual Production and Reproduction
from* Beowulf *to* Maus

THOMAS A. BREDEHOFT

OXFORD
UNIVERSITY PRESS

OXFORD

UNIVERSITY PRESS

Great Clarendon Street, Oxford, OX2 6DP,
United Kingdom

Oxford University Press is a department of the University of Oxford.
It furthers the University's objective of excellence in research, scholarship,
and education by publishing worldwide. Oxford is a registered trade mark of
Oxford University Press in the UK and in certain other countries

Published in the United States of America by Oxford University Press
198 Madison Avenue, New York, NY 10016, United States of America

British Library Cataloguing in Publication Data
Data available

Library of Congress Control Number: 2013942188

ISBN 978-0-19-960316-9 (hbk.)
978-0-19-960315-2 (pbk.)

Printed by
CPI Group (UK) Ltd, Croydon, CRO 4YY

SERIES EDITORS' PREFACE

Oxford Textual Perspectives is a new series of informative and provocative studies focused upon texts (conceived of in the broadest sense of that term) and the technologies, cultures, and communities that produce, inform, and receive them. It provides fresh interpretations of fundamental works, images, and artefacts, and of the vital and challenging issues emerging in English literary studies. By engaging with the contexts and materiality of the text, its production, transmission, and reception history, and by frequently testing and exploring the boundaries of the notions of text and meaning themselves, the volumes in the series question conventional frameworks and provide innovative interpretations of both canonical and less well-known works. These books will offer new perspectives, and challenge familiar ones, both on and through texts and textual communities. While they focus on specific authors, periods, and issues, they nonetheless scan wider horizons, addressing themes and provoking questions that have a more general application to literary studies and cultural history as a whole. Each is designed to be as accessible to the non-specialist reader as it is fresh and rewarding for the specialist, combining an informative orientation in a landscape with detailed analysis of the territory and suggestions for further travel.

Elaine Treharne and *Greg Walker*

ACKNOWLEDGEMENTS

The conception and composition of this book has followed an unusual course, and I suspect that even I do not remember all those friends and colleagues who have contributed to it. The following folks, however, have made individual contributions that deserve to be spelled out specifically. So:

Thanks to Elaine Treharne, for giving me the confidence and encouragement to write it in the first place, though it has taken me far outside my comfort zone. Thanks to Harold Forbes, at the WVU library, for granting me such easy access to that university's set of Shakespeare folios. Thanks to Ryan Claycomb, for without his timely intervention, much of the argument would have taken a radically different form. Thanks to Pat Conner, who graciously allowed me to bend his ear about virtually all the ideas contained herein, as well as about other topics, over many cups of coffee. Thanks also to Brian Luskey and Kate Staples, for their useful responses to a messy early draft of two chapters. And a somewhat more diffuse but no less heartfelt thanks to Dan Donoghue, Siân Echard, Janet Ericksen, Martin Foys, Erin Jordan, Michael Kramp, Chris Jones, Drew Jones, Stacy Klein, Roy Liuzza, Leslie Lockett, Jo Story, and Elizabeth Tyler, for friendship and fellowship at conferences, or in your homes, or over email, and in other ways: your support and scepticism both have profited this book. Thanks in every possible way, as well, to Rosemary Hathaway, whose patience and support through these six stressful years (some parts of which have been focused on this book) have been worth all the rest.

CONTENTS

LIST OF ILLUSTRATIONS

Introduction

A mong the many Anglo-Saxon treasures of the British Museum is the small eighth-century whalebone chest now usually known as the Franks Casket. Intricately carved on all four sides as well as on a top panel, the Casket shows scenes from Christian history, from Germanic legend, and from the Bible, attesting to the complex cultural forces operating in Anglo-Saxon England at the time; each of the four sides includes written material, in either English runes, Latin letters, or both, generally relating to the accompanying images. The right-hand side of the Casket features a puzzling set of cryptic runes, seemingly involving a vowel-substitution cipher of some sort: where we might expect to see vowels there only appear to be more consonants. The cipher was, it is widely agreed, 'solved' in an important 1900 essay by Arthur Napier, who identified cryptic forms of the Old English vowels 'a', 'æ', 'e', 'i', and 'o'.[1] Napier's solution was widely adopted and forms the basis for the standard edition of the text in the *Anglo-Saxon Poetic Records*:

> Her Hos sitæþ   on hærmbergæ
> agl[.] drigiþ,   swæ hiri Ertae gisgraf
> særden sorgæ   and sefa tornæ.

---

[1] Arthur Napier, 'Contributions to Old English Literature: 1. An Old English Homily on the Observance of Sunday. 2. The Franks Casket', in W. P. Ker, A. S. Napier, and W. W. Skeat, eds., *An English Miscellany presented to Dr F. J. Furnivall* (reprint edn. New York: AMS, 1969), pp. 355–81.

('Here sits Hos on the harm-barrow; she endures *agl[.]*, as Ertae appointed to her a sore-den of sorrows and troubles of mind.')[2] Napier literally made the cryptic text legible, but a damaged letter and some difficult words have meant that its meaning has remained an open question in some ways.

For over a century, scholars studying the Casket have read the cryptic right-hand text with the aid of Napier's solution, but it now appears to be the case that Napier's solution was incomplete. In a recent essay, I have shown that an additional cryptic rune-consonant should be read as the vowel 'u', changing three characters previously understood as 'r'.[3] Although one resulting word, 'sæuden', remains difficult to construe, the prepositional phrase 'on hærmbergæ' should now be read 'on hæum bergæ' (on the high hill) and the otherwise unknown proper name 'Ertae' can now be properly read as 'Eutae', seeming to reference the tribal name of the Jutes recorded in the Venerable Bede's *Historia ecclesiastica* as well as in the poem *Beowulf*. Although not all modern scholars assent to an origin for *Beowulf* in Bede's eighth-century Northumbrian milieu, the Franks Casket's date and Northumbrian dialect open the door for a reinterpretation of this puzzling bit of verse in just such a context.

I begin with this example because it exposes a central problem in the very process of what we know as reading, which can be understood as a process for decrypting the mysterious signs we call letters into meaningful language. Once Napier had done the initial work of decoding the Casket's cryptic runes, later generations of readers could well argue about the meaning of the language that Napier had found within the inscription, but once it had been read, scholars effectively ceased to look at the runic material itself, preferring to read through it to the bit of language they understood it to conceal. What this example teaches us so clearly is that we often conceptualize reading as an operation that is somehow directly opposed to seeing: although we must of course see a text that we read (and I refer here only to the common case, and pass

---

[2] George Philip Krapp and Elliott V. K. Dobbie, eds., *The Anglo-Saxon Poetic Records* [ASPR], 6 vols. (New York: Columbia University Press, 1931–53), vol. 6: *The Anglo-Saxon Minor Poems*, p. 116. The translation is mine, as are all translations into Modern English throughout, unless otherwise noted.

[3] Thomas A. Bredehoft, 'Three New Cryptic Runes on the Franks Casket', *Notes and Queries* N.S. 58.2 (2011), 181–3.

over exceptions such as Braille writing), the very process of reading assigns importance or significance not to the visible aspects of letters, but to the linguistic entities that lie behind them. Once we reach beyond the visible signs to their linguistic meanings, we feel free to discard or ignore the visible component. The visible aspect of the text is treated as a veil that conceals the meanings that we hope to find within texts, and what a cryptic text like that on the Franks Casket does is to call our attention as readers to the veil itself; here we must see as well as read.

It will be one of my central contentions in this book that we must always see as well as read, whether the text in question is overtly cryptic or not. Further, the notion that the visible component of text is able to be discarded or ignored or bypassed must be understood as an ideological position. Seemingly one of the central underpinnings of our entire practice of literacy, this ideological principle is, like writing itself, something that Jacques Derrida would label as a *pharmakon*—a drug—neither medicinal remedy nor poison, although having the potential to partake of both.[4] Writing's ability to serve as a representation of language, Derrida insists, is always accompanied by a *supplément*, an irreducible difference, or gap, or deferral, falling between the written text and its supposed linguistic content. The three 'u's conventionally (and I believe incorrectly) read as 'r' in the Franks Casket text remind us that what is lost when we cross the gap between seeing and reading can sometimes be very important indeed. But the truly important lesson here will not allow us to merely let the new reading of the Casket replace the old; rather it should remind us that reading, as a strategy or practice, must always lose something in that gap. Seeing cannot simply be a remedy (or even a *pharmakon*) for reading, it is important to recognize, as seeing no doubt leaves its own gaps and *suppléments*, but seeing while we are reading can help us recognize the play in the text.

To put it in other terms, whenever we read, we must simultaneously remain conscious of our visual experience of a text. To do so, I believe, means that we must attend closely to what it is, exactly, that we mean by the word 'text'. In this book, where I will cover materials ranging from Anglo-Saxon manuscripts and inscribed objects like the Franks Casket to modern contemporary comics works like Chris Ware's *Jimmy Corrigan*,

---

[4] Jacques Derrida, 'Plato's Pharmacy', in *Dissemination*, trans. Barbara Johnson (Chicago: University of Chicago Press, 1981), pp. 61–171.

it will become clear quite quickly that any definition of text we might choose to use necessarily leaves its own irreducible gaps and problems. To choose a definition, or even to attempt to arrive at one, is to surrender the game in some fashion, to limit the possibilities of the very project at hand, which is to articulate the necessity of both reading and seeing: defining precisely what is a 'text', I suspect, is always to return us to a paradigm of reading. Instead of offering a singular definition of 'text', then, I will offer a dual definition in order to indicate the nature of my arguments as we proceed through the chapters of this book: on the one hand, as we shall see, a text is a media object, that which is reproduced or otherwise caught up within an economy of reproduction; on the other hand, a text must be understood as that which is bounded and defined by paratext. Much of the history that my own book will attempt to trace can be understood as what falls in the gap between and beyond these two competing definitions.

Textual media and the logic of the copy

As part of his fascinating close reading of Plato's *Phaedrus*, Derrida both articulates and undermines what we can conveniently label 'the logic of the copy' or 'the logic of copying'. In those domains where the logic of the copy operates, one understands that by its very nature the copy is always a failure, and what it fails at specifically is to be identical to what it attempts to reproduce. Derrida, primarily concerned with ideas that swirl around writing as a secondary phenomenon, an implicit or explicit attempt to represent speech or language, suggests that the ideological content of the logic of the copy misunderstands or misrepresents the play that characterizes writing: 'Having no essence, introducing difference as the condition for the presence of essence, opening up the possibility of the double, the copy, the imitation, the simulacrum—the game and the *graphē* are constantly disappearing as they go along.'[5] Thus, for Derrida, critiques of writing that characterize it as a failure simply reinscribe a claim that is essentially ideological in nature. Yet if one can step outside of that ideological formation, writing need not be a failure and

---

[5] Derrida, 'Plato's Pharmacy', p. 157.

what we might be inclined to call a text need not be seen as a copy or representation of anything at all, but can rather be a thing in itself.

In principle, Derrida's insight allows us to distinguish between scripts that are subject to the logic of the copy (texts, media) and those which are not, although we do not have any equivalently convenient label for the latter category; I will generally call such items textual artefacts or productions. The act of distinguishing between texts and textual artefacts, however, seems difficult, especially when our most basic notion of reading means, of course, to use the script to grant us access to its linguistic contents: in its most basic formation, and perhaps even in its historically originary formation, reading means reading aloud, and reading aloud explicitly generates language itself. In other words, the act of reading (aloud) appears always to position the script as medial: certainly the script lies outside the reader, and to the degree that it also lies outside the writer, the script seems inherently medial.

Yet from a very early stage indeed, some scripts clearly exploit the gap or *supplément* between their written form and the linguistic content they generate or contain. To return to the example of the cryptic inscription on the right-hand side of the Franks Casket, Napier's conventional reading of the second verse as 'on hærmbergæ' ('on the harm-barrow') and my own revised reading of the same verse as 'on hæum bergæ' ('on the high hill') both accomplish the work of translating the carved or inscribed runes into speakable language. Lost in both translations, of course, whether we put them into speech or alternative alphabets, are the visual similarities and differences between the two r-shaped runes that lead to the different readings. Yet those similarities and differences are an essential component of the Franks Casket, and the operation of turning the inscription into either speakable language or a non-runic alphabet must either erase the differences (Napier's reading) or the similarities (my reading). In short, the process of reading this passage insistently treats the Franks Casket's cryptic text as medial: to read the cryptic text (aloud) means to treat the inscription as standing between us and a piece of language that can be vocalized or transcribed.

Let me rephrase that. The act of reading the cryptic passage means to treat it as a media object, a text, despite the ways in which doing so essentially demands a misrepresentation of the Casket itself. That is, the Casket is not a media object, it is not (or not merely) medial, lying between us and a piece of language that we hope to access. The runes of the Franks

Casket, rather than functioning representationally, through the logic of the copy, function as the thing itself, the real. Solving the cipher of the Casket is precisely the act that allows us to treat it as medial, to literally make it into a text; before it is solved, or when we wish to focus on the act of solution, it is, essentially, not a text at all. This claim, of course, merely restates the definition of text I am currently exploring: a text is a media object, subject to the logic of the copy, both attempting to represent a passage of language and necessarily failing at that attempt. The fact that the cipher has been encoded onto the Casket by an author figure, like the fact that the Casket is positioned medially between readers and that author figure, cannot be denied; but the Casket as an object, and its script as a cipher, is more than and different from an artefact subject to the logic of the copy. By solving the cipher and (hence) reading the text, we subject it to the logic of the copy: and thus we do a kind of violence to what it is. The creator of the Casket, of course, demands that violence from us, by requiring us to solve the cipher; he or she is playing with us.

But as this very example confirms, the idea of a text as a media object, something subject to the logic of the copy, is an ideological position that does not apply in all times and places, or to all scripts or inscriptions; one of the most surprising consequences of bringing Derrida and the Franks Casket into dialogue may well be the recognition that the Casket's very kind of play also serves as a critique of this most familiar (to us) ideology of writing. In many times and places, the logic of the copy has indeed dominated the books and written materials that make up our objects of literary study, but it has not always been dominant, and the operation of the logic of the copy is very much in need of historicization.

Text and paratext

An alternative model for defining what exactly is a text is, one must admit, especially closely concerned with works of literature. The focus on the literary, however, is necessary: one of the things that literary objects do most consistently is to challenge or address the very categories that make textual activity possible, and histories of the book must always attend to literary history. This second partial definition for 'text' involves the tension between text and paratext, although just where the boundary between the two lies is not always certain. As described by Gérard Genette in the opening to his massive survey of paratextual forms,

> the paratext is what enables a text to become a book and to be offered as such to its reader and, more generally, to the public. More than a boundary or a sealed border, the paratext is, rather, a *threshold*, or—a word Borges used apropos of a preface—a 'vestibule' that offers the possibility of either stepping inside or turning back.[6]

Genette, while especially concerned with books and publishers in the print era, acknowledges that paratexts have functioned variously across time, and that they might apply as well to much shorter texts than those which make up books. But even in his incredibly brief introductory list, 'an author's name, a title, a preface, illustrations,'[7] Genette signals to readers just what paratexts are as well as what they do: paratexts do the work of identification, location, contextualization, and definition that give a text its unique identity.

Genette's further association between paratexts and the process of publication—which implies, of course, reproduction of the text, marking it explicitly as subject to the logic of the copy—reveals the surprising interdependence of my 'paratextual' and the 'media' definitions of text. Even more surprising, perhaps, is the extraordinarily long history of this association between paratextual apparatus and textual reproduction, as we shall see in Chapter 1. Texts tend to be accompanied by paratexts *and* to participate in an economy of reproduction that positions them as medial, and this connection existed long before the invention of printing.

An example can clarify what is at stake here. In many contexts, the familiar phrase 'To err is human; to forgive, divine' functions as a proverb, a frozen expression communicating a bit of conventional wisdom. Conversely, to identify it as line 525 of Alexander Pope's *Essay on Criticism* is to associate it with a powerful set of paratexts: an author's name, a title, and a set of boundaries denoted here by line numbers. Further, to identify it as a quotation explicitly places it within the realm of reproduction: a quotation is always a (partial, thus faulty) copy for which there is an identifiable, authoritative original. In a very real sense, however,

---

[6] Gérard Genette, *Paratexts: Thresholds of Interpretation*, trans. Jane E. Lewin (Cambridge: Cambridge University Press, 1987), pp. 1–2.

[7] Genette, *Paratexts*, p. 1.

the deployment of this phrase as a proverb takes place outside the logic of the copy: as a proverb, it functions as the thing itself, not merely as a reproduction of some 'original' version of itself. Likewise, as a proverb, 'To err is human' has no author; as conventional wisdom, it is the common property of us all, and in popular discourse it does not function as a quotation from Pope, regardless of its probable origin. Our ability to trace the history of 'To err is human' merely exposes our ability as readers to make the proverb into a text—precisely by associating it with a suite of paratextual materials. While there is, at some linguistic level, no difference between 'To err is human; to forgive, divine' when used as a proverb and when used as a quotation from Pope, the paratextual and medial issues addressed here make it worthwhile indeed for us to label the differences that do exist, and those very paratextual and reproductive issues indicate that only the quotation actually functions as a text.

This process of making something into a text by associating it with a title, an author's name, and other paratextual apparatus has been an exceptionally useful strategy for authors, book makers, publishers, and literary readers through the centuries, and I have no intention to deny either its usefulness or its power.[8] But it seems important to note that a process that makes things into texts must, indeed, start with raw materials that are not in fact texts. What an understanding of how texts are defined by their paratexts allows us to do is to recognize texts when we find them, as well as at least tentatively identify some things (like the proverb version of 'To err is human') that might appropriately be understood as non-texts, at some level. While contemporary literary and cultural studies might feel comfortable with seeing everything as a text, it is important to be explicitly aware of when something is a text by its very nature, and when it is that we make something into a text for our own convenience and purposes.

A first effort

My discussion so far has been brief, but it has attempted a great deal: to insist on the necessity of seeing as well as reading; to note that reading

---

[8] On the author's name in particular, see Michel Foucault, 'What is an Author?', in Paul Rabinow, ed., *The Foucault Reader* (New York: Pantheon, 1984), pp. 101–20.

as a strategy serves to make whatever it consumes into texts; and to suggest that a text is a specific kind of textual object (for lack of a better term) that generally operates as subject to the logic of the copy, or is accompanied by a defining paratext, or both. These claims, of course, are interlinked, enchained one from another, and they stand at the heart of the analysis that will be used throughout my book. As such, I think it is useful here to work out some of the implications of these starting points in some detail in order to clarify the directions later chapters will take. At the risk of seeming perverse, I shall consider three examples, from quite different ends of the tradition of English letters; my examples are all linked to one another by their use of retrograde letters.

Retrograde letters, of course, 'walk backwards', and my first example of retrograde script also derives from the Franks Casket (Figure 1), which I discussed in some detail above. In addition to the right side, where the runic script is obscured for readers by the use of a complex set of cryptic runes in a vowel-substitution cipher, the front side of the Casket exhibits a text that (according to the conventional reading) extends through the four panels surrounding the central images, beginning at the upper left, continuing down the right-hand side, proceeding in retrograde fashion across the bottom panel, and then (abandoning the retrograde orientation of the characters) back up the left-hand panel.[9] The images show, on the left half, a scene from the Germanic legend of Weland the smith (in which Weland offers his captor a drinking cup), and on the right, the Christian Adoration of the Magi. The poetic passage seems to have nothing to do with these images, however, and reads, according to the standard transcription, as:

> Fisc flodu ahof   on fergenberig;
> warþ gasric grorn,   þær he on greut giswom.
> Hronæs ban.

('The fish threw water onto the mighty mountain; the gusher-powerful one grew sad where he swam upon the gravel. Whale's bone.' The entire

---

[9] On the right-hand side and left-hand side of the three-dimensional Casket, runic texts in the bottom panel appear inverted, but not retrograde (that is, the script reads left to right when the box itself is inverted). On the right-hand side, of course, the result is both inverted and cryptographic text. The back side does not have a continuous text panel across the bottom.

second poetic line stands as the retrograde portion.)[10] Structurally, the text seems almost to be riddle and answer, with two lines of poetry, followed by a two-word, non-metrical phrase presented at the end, apparently as a kind of summation. Yet the words 'whale's bone' in the fourth panel are usually taken as a reference to the material of the Casket itself, and they seem to have no clear reference to the poetic lines, other than that the fish of the poem and the whale must be the same. Likewise, the poetic lines themselves do not really seem like a riddle, although 'gasric' is a problematic word, and there is some uncertainty over subject and object in the first clause. The real riddle would seem to be the relationship among the parts: the Germanic and Christian stories in the images; the poetic lines; the explicit presence of the 'solution' to the riddle in the words 'whale's bone'.

It is at least possible, I suspect, that the solution to the riddle posed by the Franks Casket's front side is not 'hronæs ban' but 'hronæs bana': 'whale's slayer', or, somewhat more archaically, 'whale's bane'. Such a

---

[10] Krapp and Dobbie, eds., *The Anglo-Saxon Minor Poems*, ASPR, vol. 6, p. 116.

reading is literally retrograde, as it asks readers to read backwards (to the extent of a single rune), effectively doubling the 'a' of 'ban' to read 'bana'. But 'whale's bane' feels like a riddling 'solution' to the two poetic lines that is much more effective than 'whale's bone': the scene in which the beached whale struggles upon the shingle (whether lifted by the flood onto the rocks or dashing the water against the hillside in its struggles) is riddlingly solved or resolved by the invocation of the death of the whale far more effectively than by the reference to its bone. The relationship between bane and bone, between death and Casket, may also suggest that the death of the whale was like a gift to the carver, and the gift-giving images involving Weland and the Magi would then also fit into such a reading.[11]

But even hypothesizing such a solution to the complex of text and images on this side of the Casket reveals the difficulties in reading caused by this sort of textualized language play. Here, the retrograde runes open up the otherwise linear reading of the text to the possibility of a bi-linear reading; the carved images likewise play off each other as well as off the text, which has its own image-like qualities emphasized here. Even the nature of the writing support—the whalebone—is meaningful here, and the riddle simply cannot be solved if we focus only upon the linguistic content of the script: the Franks Casket is a textual artefact, but the riddle on its front panel cannot simply be read as a text. To clarify, if both 'ban' and 'bana' are operative on the Casket, the one-to-one equation between runic sign and linguistic signified is explicitly interrupted in such a way as to highlight the very ideological importance of that equation in the process of reading texts. In that sense, it is not a text, in that it is not really medial, standing between us and a particular bit of language. Simultaneously, its general lack of paratexts (unless we choose to see the images as merely paratextual) is part of the Casket's non-text status. But the images are not, in my reading, illustrative or paratextual: they serve not as a threshold or vestibule, as a liminal boundary point allowing access to the text, but as something much more integral and even (literally) central.

---

[11] On gift-giving and the Franks Casket, see Richard Abels, 'What Has Weland to Do with Christ? The Franks Casket and the Acculturation of Christianity in Early Anglo-Saxon England', *Speculum* 84 (2009), 549–81.

Similarly, my second example (Figure 2), from Chris Ware's 2003 collection, *Quimby the Mouse*, uses visual material that cannot be seen as paratextual.[12] Written and drawn as a one-page comic, it is not clear even whether this comic is titled, as the apparent title 'I'm a Very Generous Person' may well simply be part of the text, if we can identify the linguistic component of a comic by that label. Ware's comic makes use of two of his most characteristic concerns and strategies: the architectural effect of the comics page and the use of lettering as a visually communicative structure in its own right, as distinct from (or supplemental to) the linguistic content of the words.[13] Within the panels, we see one side of a pair of telephone conversations, but surrounding them is a series of headings both normal, retrograde, and in various orientations, suggesting a probable reading something like 'I'm a very generous person, but I just can't stand being around you anymore; you make me happy sometimes though…I guess…Uh…I can't stand being alone.' To arrive at such a reading, the reader must negotiate text that runs left to right, right to left, retrograde, down, and doubled (if that is the right word): 'you' appears once, but must be read twice, recalling my doubled reading of the a-rune on the Franks Casket's 'ban'/'bana'. 'I can't stand' must also be read twice, once in a sentence organized horizontally, and once in a sentence built vertically.

Further, Ware's headings combine outline effects, solid-coloured letters, and white letters against a coloured background, in three colours of ink (black, blue, and red), sometimes with words in two colours occupying the same physical space on the page. These strategies are explicitly structured by the multi-colour printing process that contextualizes his form, and the whole 'crooked house' built by Quimby's phone dialogue is implied by the overall composition of the panels and their surround. The linguistic construction of this particular crooked house is playfully indicated by the 'T' in 'BUT', where one of the Quimby figures pounds

---

[12] F. C. Ware, *Quimby the Mouse* (Seattle: Fantagraphics, 2003), p. 56.

[13] On architecture and architectural metaphors as structuring principles of Chris Ware's work, see Thomas A. Bredehoft, 'Comics Architecture, Multidimensionality, and Time: Chris Ware's *Jimmy Corrigan: The Smartest Kid on Earth*', *Mfs* 52.4 (2006), 869–90. On Ware's use of lettering and visual design, see Gene Kannenberg, 'The Comics of Chris Ware: Text, Image, and Visual Narrative Strategies', in Robin Varnum and Christina T. Gibbons, eds., *The Language of Comics: Word and Image* (Jackson, MS: University Press of Mississippi, 2001), pp. 174–97.

FIG 2   F. C. Ware, 'I'm a Very Generous Person'.

Image courtesy of Chris Ware. Copyright © 2014 Chris Ware.

the 'T' as if it were a nail. Here text becomes image and image becomes text most transparently. But, of course, comics works generally cannot be understood as containing 'text' and 'image' as separate and separable components, which is one of Ware's points here: the words are (also) pictures and the pictures are not mere paratextual appendages to (or definers of) 'the text'. Indeed, the degree to which this particular comics page operates without obvious paratext is notable, although the book it appears in does have a title clearly attached (the author's name is, however, very difficult to find, although present). But here, where the central design of the comics page is a house, neither words nor images serve merely as a 'vestibule', the structure of the whole being made indivisibly of both.

My final example of retrograde words comes from Mark Danielewski's 2000 novel, *House of Leaves*.[14] On page 140 of the novel, we find two sorts of retrograde text: within a central box (which is outlined in blue ink), we find a retrograde list of architectural terms; surrounding the box is footnote 183, both retrograde and rotated ninety degrees from its normal orientation. Footnote 183, continued in similar fashion on pages 142 and 144, contains a lengthy list of documentary films, and it is appended to the end of footnote 182 (a list of documentary filmmakers) which itself ends on page 141. Page 140, of course, is the verso side of page 139; the central retrograde box on page 140, readers of the novel will notice, repeats text that is presented in normal orientation in a similar box on the recto side (page 139). Specifically, the blue-bounded box on this leaf (and the novel's title, *House of Leaves*, specifically references the leaves of books) encloses identical text printed in normal orientation on the recto, and printed retrograde on the verso: the effect is to present the illusion of transparency, as if the letters we see inside the blue box on 140 are the very letters on 139, but now seen from behind. Yet in the copy of the book I am working with as I write this, the printing on the two sides of the page is slightly off-register; holding the page to the light reveals the near-opaqueness of the printed paper page as well as the imperfect registering of the texts.

It seems clear that Danielewski's novel plays these textual and typographical games in part to ask readers to consider and confront the differences between print textuality and virtual (computer screen)

---

[14] Mark Danielewski, *House of Leaves* (New York: Pantheon, 2000).

textuality: the blue-bounded box on these pages has some of the effect of a monitor or screen, imaginatively seen from opposite sides. It is striking, however, how these textual games are situated within a larger structure that is metaphorically architectural in nature. The emphasis on houses in particular, in both the Ware and Danielewski examples, seems to align both of them with the manifest three-dimensionality of the Franks Casket: in all three examples, retrograde writing is explicitly or metaphorically presented in an architectural context.[15] Though it cannot be certain, the current reconstruction of the Franks Casket may be incorrect. Reconstructed now with the top panel placed at right angles to all four side panels, it seems at least possible it might be reconstructed with the current top panel being positioned as the only survivor from a pair of panels arranged in a gabled fashion. Such a reconstruction would give the Casket a house shape, just as the Gandersheim reliquary (to which the Franks Casket is sometimes compared) is house-shaped.

But it is important also to work through some of *House of Leaves*'s play with issues of paratextuality more fully. Danielewski's novel, for example, presents itself as the second edition of a book originally published on the Internet, a book edited by one Johnny Truant, from the papers left after the death of an old man named Zampanò, who had constructed an elaborate narrative around an apparently non-existent documentary film, *The Navidson Record*, which, in turn, was based upon some home movies of an unusual house. These fictionalized layers of authorial, editorial, and publishing intervention are reflected in prefaces, footnotes, illustrations, appendices, and other conventional paratextual apparatus within which the retrograde footnotes and other textual strategies seen on page 140 are not even especially unusual. Positioned at the boundary between printed text and electronic text, *House of Leaves* serves (among other things) as a kind of postmodern encyclopaedia of paratextual strategies, playing with the ways in which authors' names, titles, notes, and so on defer meaning and significance even as they seem to certify them.

As all three of my examples suggest, retrograde writing not only challenges our basic understanding of writing as linear, but also appears to open the door for challenges to the tabularity or two-dimensionality of

---

[15] See Elaine Treharne, 'The Architextual Editing of Early English', *Poetica* 71 (2009), 1–13.

the page.[16] In this sense, retrograde script also seems to serve—at least in these examples—to urge readers to do more than consume the text by merely reading or seeing: the emphasis on three-dimensionality in these examples also raises physical, even tactile issues. Even if only in the imagination, a careful reader must hold Danielewski's page up to the light, a careful reader of Ware's comic must rotate the book to read the text, and the various sides and text-panels of the Franks Casket cannot all be read or even seen at once. Yet in each case, short of actually using a mirror, no amount of re-orienting these books and objects can make the retrograde text legible in the ordinary manner: retrograde text itself reminds us that the act of reading a three-dimensional book or object always involves an equally potent, even if only imagined, act of re-orientation. That is, the retrograde text reminds us of and foregrounds the physicality of writing itself, as it reminds us of the mental gymnastics we so readily perform to make sense of the seemingly or supposedly one-dimensional linear text. Reading is not transparent, these examples insist, but a complex mode of interpreting the visible.

Further, it seems important to emphasize that, while my examples were chosen as examples of retrograde texts, each also shows both some relationship to architectural or three-dimensional visuality and a probable example of doubled reading that serves as an additional challenge to linearity: 'bana' for 'ban' on the Franks Casket; the words 'I can't stand' in Ware's comic; the list of architectural terms in Danielewski's novel. Influence between or among any of these examples seems very unlikely; the similarities seen among these texts reveal a crucial set of homologies that cross virtually the entire chronological range of English literary expression and that demand our attention. And while this book cannot trace all such continuities or homologies, I hope to trace one axis upon which we can hang at least a partial understanding of these texts' investment in issues of visuality and legibility.

When contrasted to normally oriented script (as in all three of my examples), retrograde script actively resists any attempt to read it, as any attempt to read it aloud must attest. Anyone who speaks aloud the text upon the Franks Casket or in Chris Ware's comic necessarily sequences

---

[16] I owe this use of the term 'tabularity' to Christian Vandendorpe, *From Papyrus to Hypertext: Towards the Universal Digital Library* (Urbana: University of Illinois Press, 2009).

the phonemes, insisting upon a linear order and significance that literally ignores or bypasses the retrograde orientation, as well as sometimes reading twice what appears only once. Likewise, reading *House of Leaves* aloud would confront the reader with innumerable problems of sequencing and linearity that would do equal violence to the physicality of that book. Precisely by urging readers to pass over their visual reversal (the visible signifier) to leap directly to their linguistic component (the signified), retrograde characters foreground and undermine the very structural principle which founds writing itself. Small wonder, then, that retrograde texts, as analysed here, often accompany challenges to other structural features of writing as well. Similarly, no possible edition of these retrograde texts can fully capture or represent their unique features, because editions by their very nature necessarily place textual material into some reproductive medium and subject it to the logic of the copy. As I will suggest further in Chapter 3, even the most faithful facsimile cannot escape the logic of the copy: these retrograde texts explicitly challenge the ideological claims of the logic of the copy, regardless of whether they (like the Franks Casket) remind us of the necessity of encountering the thing itself or (like Ware and Danielewski) expose certain failures of the logic of the copy from within the paradigm of printed reproduction itself. To a remarkable degree, the homologies involved here—not only in the use of retrograde characters, but also in the associated challenges to linearity, tabularity, and the logic of the copy in particular—present themselves as more or less explicit challenges to the structural operation and ideology of writing itself. It is difficult not to conclude that the investment of all three examples in houses and architecture is not itself a commentary upon, or a challenge to, the very defining metaphor of structure itself.

Going forward

What my discussion of these examples of retrograde script accomplishes, I hope, is to demonstrate the usefulness of understanding more clearly how my intertwined definitions of 'text' as medial, on the one hand, and as defined by paratext, on the other, can help us to both read and see texts and textual productions. In the chapters which follow, I will attempt to begin the work of historicization which is implied in the preceding discussion: to the degree that the homologies and parallels discussed above attest to a kind of recurring critique of the dominant ideology of writing within the tradition of English letters, one aspect of my history must trace a kind of historical continuity in how books and authors understand the nature of writing itself. But the equally manifest differences in my examples (such as how they are all more or less explicitly shaped by the technologies of their production: whalebone carving; coloured printing; computer-mediated print) indicate the necessity of a historical narrative that attends to difference as well, perhaps with a special emphasis on technological developments.

I begin, then, in the first chapter, with an assessment of the general state of affairs during the Anglo-Saxon period. Starting with the eighth century, the very period in which the Franks Casket was produced, I consider two quite different examples that attest to two competing ideologies behind the production of manuscript books during the period. The first, exemplified by the Venerable Bede and his magnificent *Historia ecclesiastica gentis Anglorum*, seems utterly familiar: Bede understands the dissemination of his work as taking place within an economy of reproduction, and he seems fully aware indeed of the operation of the logic of the copy. Bede's contemporary Boniface, on the other hand, engages in a lengthy correspondence with various figures in Anglo-Saxon England about their ability to supply him with manuscript books: nowhere does Boniface, however, seem to ever consider the logic of the copy as applying to the books he produces or receives: as far as Boniface seems to be concerned, each manuscript is a unique individual production: a valuable and authoritative book in itself, rather than sometimes being a mere flawed 'copy'. The bulk of Chapter 1 attempts to trace the implications of the concurrent existence of both ideological positions and how they leave their traces in the books and works that survive to our time.

Specifically, Chapter 1 argues that a suite of paratextual strategies, including the name of the author, a clear definition of textual boundaries, and often an authorial preface as well, were clearly associated in Anglo-Saxon England with a perspective on textuality that was centred around textual reproduction as a paradigm. Simultaneously, the frequent appearance of anonymous works (and works lacking similar paratextual apparatus in general) can be seen as deriving from an alternative ideological perspective, one which I will suggest was actually dominant throughout the period. This second ideological position understands the production of each and every individual book as an act of production, not reproduction, just as the making of the Franks Casket was an act of production. The evidence for the importance, even predominance, of this ideology is varied and widespread, and the implications for our understanding of Anglo-Saxon literature and culture are radical indeed. The central claim of Chapter 1 might be phrased in intentionally provocative terms: *Beowulf*, I will suggest, is not a text. Not only does *Beowulf* lack almost the entire paratextual apparatus that can give definition to a text, but there is little or no evidence of its participation in an economy of reproduction until well into the modern print era. *Beowulf* should be seen as a unique artefact, rather than a copy of anything at all, despite the ease with which modern readers pull it relentlessly into the realm of texts by doing things like giving it a title or reading it as medial. *Beowulf*, like many Anglo-Saxon manuscript works, is more like the Franks Casket than like Bede's *Historia*.

In my second chapter, focused on the Gothic period (roughly from 1100 to 1500), I will suggest that a cultural transformation occurred in the twelfth century, leading to the predominance of the reproductive ideology over the productive ideology, although the latter never died out entirely. The implications of this shift are widespread, and they affected authors from Geoffrey of Monmouth to Chaucer, as well as shaping book production well into the print era. Under the Gothic paradigm of reproduction, copies were first made (and the word *copia* is associated with manuscript copies only from the thirteenth century on). But where Derrida appears to understand that the very act of writing involves the imagination of an ideal, transcendental original, Gothic culture seems to make no such defining association. Indeed, the central feature of Gothic reproduction seems to be an understanding that two copies of a single original will necessarily differ from one another, without either necessarily invalidating the authority of the other. Rather than being an ideal original, a transcendent signifier, the original in Gothic culture is understood as a moving target, either utterly inaccessible or shifting and multiform. Late medieval textual *variance*, at every level from the word to the structure of a book, reflects this 'moving target' understanding of the Gothic original, and the literary figures of translation and dream also seem caught up in this new Gothic ideology.

Importantly, this mode of Gothic reproduction appears not to have been limited to textual culture, but can also be seen in Gothic architecture, stained glass, and even in mass-produced items like pilgrim badges. Gothic visual culture, then, becomes especially important for reminding us not to focus too exclusively on texts, which give us only one side of a more complex story. The way that the variation-within-repetition dynamic that drives the Gothic aesthetic applies both in books and literature as well as in other areas of visual culture reminds us that, even in the Gothic period, literary culture was not completely separated from visual culture. Regardless, the central and defining notion that books (and other items) were, indeed, copies or reproductions serves to indicate that we are solidly into the realm of media, and that Gothic mediation ultimately made the printing press possible.

The invention of the printing press, of course, enabled a kind of tectonic shift, and the grounding of that shift seems to have lain in the ways in which print defines and conceptualizes itself as always-already a mode of reproduction. In that sense, print reproduction involves an essential continuity with the Gothic period, where reproduction already dominated. But from very early indeed, print ideologically denies the variation-within-reproduction dynamic that characterized the Gothic period, by insisting (despite its manifest untruth) that all printed copies are textually identical. From here, it is a very short step indeed to the principle that there is an ideal, or best, version of the text that ought to underlie and underwrite printed copies. Print reproduction is, ultimately, essentially defined by that notion of an ideal text, one existing only in the realm of ideas, and to the degree that the practices of print have shaped our more generalized understanding of what 'text' and 'language' do, print reproduction can indeed seem like the paradigmatic type of textuality, because of the way it foregrounds the logic of copying.

My argument in Chapter 3 suggests that the ideologically central type of printed text takes the form of what I call 'the edition', whether or not an editor plays an explicit role in its articulation. What editions do is to redeploy paratexts (including prefaces, titles, and authors' names) not in order to place a work into the realm of reproduction (which would be redundant, since all printed works are reproduced by definition), but rather to assert or insist upon the authority or authenticity or value of the printed text. That is, paratexts, in the printed domain, serve as a kind of *pharmakon* or remedy for the manifest failures of print, which derive directly from the logic of the copy. The ways in which editions locate authority or authenticity outside the text, further, open the door for a second kind of edition, the facsimile, which might at first appear to be a whole new kind of book or text. But as I argue, while the facsimile does remediate the edition, it does so ultimately in an attempt to make authenticity or authority itself visible; the facsimile cannot exist, it appears, without the edition's very lack of authenticity, and thus facsimiles, at least as we know them now, simply re-articulate the ideological logic of editions, serving to insist once more upon the authority or authenticity of a printed edition by promising to bring us close to the source of the printed edition's authority.

The most striking aspect of facsimiles, their function as reproductions organized in two dimensions, rather than linearly, brings us to the subject of my fourth chapter, comics. Comics works, I suggest, share one aspect of print's essential, ideological relationship to reproduction: just as printed text must be reproduced to count as printed, so too do comics texts need to be reproduced to count as comics. Further, comics are defined by the logic of juxtaposition across or within two dimensions, an essential difference from the ideological linearity of print, which identifies the work subject to reproduction as a work in language. Remarkably, the two-dimensional nature of comics seems to usher in a different tectonic shift, one as radical in its effects as the printing press itself. Comics works, I suggest, are generally incompatible with any understanding of the comics original as ideal, in the realm of ideas. Works in comics are, quite straightforwardly, born-printed texts, and the original artwork that may precede the printing of a work of comics is merely preliminary, not an authoritative original that can be only imperfectly reproduced. In comics, reproduction and production are simultaneous, and the original (which, indeed, may be multiplied by the hundreds or thousands) lies irresistibly in the realm of the real.

Even more intriguingly, as the printing process occasioned the reconfiguration of the function and meaning of paratexts, the unique features of comics textuality open the door for further restructuring of the roles and functioning of paratexts. And while it may be too early in the history of comics to be certain, contemporary comics works appear to suggest that comics irresistibly pull even the most mechanical of paratexts (title pages, copyright pages, cover artwork, and publishers' blurbs) into the ideological realm of text. Comics have the potential to eliminate a true distinction between text and paratext in a way that appears to be essentially new on the scene. Ultimately, my discussion of comics, however, also operates to retroactively allow us to recognize the degree to which two-dimensional structures of meaning have long contested the linearity of language and the ideological linearity of printed texts. What an understanding of comics allows is a fuller understanding of books as real, material things, as opposed to mere faulty representations of the true object of reading. As such, the importance of comics, as a reproductive mode that operates very differently from typographic print, stretches far beyond comics works themselves.

As even this brief summary indicates, the chapters that follow will cover a great deal of the history of English literature. Central themes will involve the visible experience of texts, the ways in which textual production and reproduction configured themselves in relation to the available technologies, and the ways in which literature responds to the ideologies of its own production and reproduction. That my discussion ends with the irreducible materialism of comics, intriguingly, echoes the essential materialism of the Anglo-Saxon period, and it is to that beginning that my first chapter now turns.

| 1 |

Anglo-Saxon Textual Production

I begin the investigation of Anglo-Saxon textuality that makes up this chapter with two well-known facts. First, *Beowulf* (like most classical Old English poems) survives to the present day in only a single manuscript. Second, *Beowulf* (like most classical Old English poems) has no original title, no ascription of authorship, no prefatory material, no early glossing or commentary: none of the paratextual appendages of the kind catalogued by Genette and that serve to ease or hamper readers' entry into a text. Traditionally, scholars have seen these two facts as central and significant, but essentially unrelated. It will be my argument in this chapter that there is a necessary and meaningful link between *Beowulf*'s uniqueness and its lack of paratexts.

The nature of the link, I believe, is precisely the same as the link between the two competing and complementary definitions of 'text' that I offered above. *Beowulf*'s lack of paratexts marks it as a non-text as insistently as its uniqueness hints at its manuscript's existence outside of any ideology of reproduction or copying. *Beowulf*, I will argue in this chapter, is a textual artefact or textual production, existing and produced without being subject to the logic of the copy. The *Beowulf* manuscript, in other words, is not a media object, in the sense that the encounters appropriate to the *Beowulf* manuscript do not position it as medial, but rather position it as an artefact that is a thing in itself that we must directly see and encounter. The same is true, the evidence will suggest, not only for non-manuscript objects like the Franks Casket, but also for a surprisingly wide range of Anglo-Saxon works, in both poetry and prose, Latin and Old English.

Simultaneously, however, a broad spectrum of Old English and Anglo-Saxon texts are, in fact, accompanied by titles, authorial ascriptions, and prefatory paratexts, and it is clear that Anglo-Saxon literary culture was conversant with texts as defined both by their paratexts and by their being subject to the logic of the copy. Thus, two ideological domains appear to have been simultaneously operative in Anglo-Saxon England. One, which we can label a 'reproductive' tradition, sees texts as medial and subject to the reproductive problems associated with the logic of the copy; the other, a 'productive' ideology, appears to envision the making of a book as a strictly productive act, no more an act of copying than the carving of a whalebone casket or the crafting of a golden jewel. The dynamic tension between these two ideologies, I suggest, is the defining feature of Anglo-Saxon textuality. The Anglo-Saxon period, it turns out, is an especially interesting historical moment, because it produces so very much textual material that operates in its original context outside of the ideological domain defined by the logic of the copy. Our widespread habit of merely reading this material—that is, of pulling it into the realm of medial texts by adding titles, prefaces, notes, and glossaries, as well as by printing it—troublingly obscures these works' very nature.

The radical nature of this argument, I fear, demands a somewhat complex exposition; I will begin by trying to think through the problem of *Beowulf*'s uniqueness. Preserved only in London, British Library, Cotton Vitellius A. xv, which was probably written in the first two decades of the eleventh century, *Beowulf* is a fortunate survival for us indeed, one of England's great contributions to world literature.[1] But it may not be the only manuscript of the poem that ever existed: if Michael Lapidge's recent argument about the archetype of *Beowulf* is correct, at least two manuscripts of *Beowulf* once existed before the surviving version of the poem was recorded, one from the early eighth century and one from around the turn of the tenth.[2] Even Kevin Kiernan's arguments for a late

---

[1] The date of the *Beowulf* manuscript has, of course, been debated, but a date around 1000 is generally agreed upon; see especially the sources cited below in notes 2 and 3.

[2] Michael Lapidge, 'The Archetype of *Beowulf*', *Anglo-Saxon England* 29 (2000), 5–41.

composition of the poem envision a prior exemplar for one or both parts of the poem.[3] One must wonder where, exactly, those earlier manuscripts are today. It is tempting to simply say they were lost or destroyed, but it is more useful, as a kind of introduction to the issues relevant to a consideration of Anglo-Saxon textuality, to hypothesize (or at least speculate) about the times and places where earlier *Beowulf* manuscripts might have been destroyed. Such hypothesizing, of course, can never be more than a thought experiment, but even so, I believe it is a useful one. The age-old problem of *Beowulf*'s uniqueness will be the carrot that (one hopes) will lead us through the maze of these lost manuscripts and their fate. We can start at the present and work our way backwards.

It seems to me unlikely that any hypothetical other copies of *Beowulf* survived only to be destroyed at any time in the last three centuries. To be sure, two world wars during the twentieth century brought about the destruction or loss of a number of manuscripts, some of them important. Likewise, N. R. Ker's indispensable *Catalogue of Manuscripts Containing Anglo-Saxon* records a handful of Old English manuscripts which do seem to have survived into the modern period but which cannot be located today.[4] None, however, is what can be characterized as a major manuscript—and if modern scholarship has turned up these traces of fragments and bits, one strongly suspects that a manuscript of a major work would surely have also left its traces. The case cannot be certain, however, as discoveries such as the Vatican fragments of two eighth-century continental Old Saxon poems (discovered in 1894) and the Middle English *Book of Margery Kempe* (identified in 1934) remind us that some important discoveries were not made until surprisingly late in the history of scholarship.[5] The disastrous 1731 Ashburnham House fire did destroy a number of books from the Cotton collection (which would later form the basis for the British Library's manuscript collection) including the only original records of other Old English poems like *The*

[3] Kevin Kiernan, *Beowulf and the Beowulf Manuscript*, revised edition (Ann Arbor: University of Michigan Press, 1996).

[4] N. R. Ker, *A Catalogue of Manuscripts Containing Anglo-Saxon* (Oxford: Clarendon Press, 1957).

[5] On the discovery of the Old Saxon *Genesis* and *Hêliand* fragments in the Vatican, see the summary in A. N. Doane, *The Saxon Genesis* (Madison: University of Wisconsin Press, 1991), pp. 3–8. On *The Book of Margery Kempe*'s discovery in 1934, see Sanford Brown Meech, ed., *The Book of Margery Kempe*, EETS o.s. 212, with prefatory note and appendices by Hope Emily Allen (Oxford: EETS, 1940), p. xxxii.

Battle of Maldon and *Seasons for Fasting*. But it seems very unlikely that other manuscripts of *Beowulf* lie behind the surviving catalogue descriptions of the pre-fire Cotton library.

Before the early eighteenth century, of course, large numbers of medieval manuscripts were broken up, often to serve as binding materials in other books, and some Old English poems are known only because their vellum was recycled in bindings: *Waldere* was almost certainly used in a binding and *Finnsburh* very likely was as well.[6] The introduction of print must have greatly multiplied the number of bookbindings needed, and the break-up of English monastic libraries after the dissolution of the monasteries in the 1530s seems to have provided additional raw material for many binders. Thus, our hypothetical other manuscripts of *Beowulf* (and other Old English poems) could well have suffered a similar fate at any time from the 1530s until about 1700, when medieval manuscripts seem to have largely (but not entirely) disappeared from binders' scrap piles. Yet we should surely attend more closely to the circumstance that *Finnsburh* and *Waldere* survived only as binding fragments: as seems to be the case with *Beowulf* and most of the poems in the other Old English poetic collections (the Junius, Exeter, and Vercelli books), these fragments of *Waldere* and *Finnsburh* (or the books they were removed from) may well have been the only manuscripts of these works to survive the middle ages. However we slice it, books with classical Old English poems simply do not show much evidence of surviving the middle ages in multiple copies

How about the later middle ages? This period, conventionally seen as a time when Old English was not much read or valued, makes an attractive hypothesis as a time when our manuscripts might have been destroyed. Yet the later we get in the middle ages, we find more (and fuller) library catalogues, few of whose entries seem to leave room for our missing *Beowulf* manuscripts. We might choose to hypothesize, of course, the destruction of both the books and the relevant catalogues, but that would be to explain the unknown by the unknown. The twelfth century or early thirteenth centuries, however, must be seen as at least a possibility: a number of early manuscripts depicted in E. A. Lowe's

---

[6] For *Waldere*, see Arne Zettersten, ed., *Waldere* (Manchester: Manchester University Press, 1979); for *Finnsburh*, see Jane Roberts, 'The *Finnsburh Fragment*, and its Lambeth Provenance', *NQ* n.s. 55.2 (2008), 122–4.

monumental photographic anthology, *Codices Latini Antiquiores*, are eighth-century or earlier books (mostly gospel books) that were recycled as flyleaves or binding materials in English books around the twelfth century (*CLA* 129, 130, 153, 154, 158, 164, 178, 232, 262, 263, 264, 1679, 1740); one eighth-century Anglo-Saxon manuscript of the gospels was recycled as a palimpsest in the thirteenth century (*CLA* 169).[7] Indeed, it seems especially likely that the *Finnsburh* fragment served as a flyleaf in Lambeth 487, which dates from precisely this period, or possibly in another book.[8]

Even so, the most likely time and place for the destruction of our hypothetical manuscripts of *Beowulf*, it seems to me, is during the Anglo-Saxon period itself, either through recycling or out and out destruction. Indeed, if we take this thought experiment to its logical conclusion, I think we end up with a scenario like the following: at some point in the early eleventh century, a good deal of time and effort, ink and vellum was dedicated to the making of a manuscript of *Beowulf* (including other works), and if Lapidge is correct, the poem was copied from an exemplar that might have been, at that time, a hundred years old or older. The making of the new *Beowulf* manuscript involved some important changes: the script was updated, in this case with a combination of two different scripts current in the first decades of the eleventh century. Likewise, much of the spelling was recast to conform with standard late West Saxon literary conventions. The resulting book was a convenient, pleasing size, suitable to be held in one hand or carried in a small bag, with a clean new look and up-to-date language. But what of the exemplar? Its size is hard to reconstruct, but it was probably old, and it manifestly would not have had a new look in terms of either script or language. Indeed, the new book was very likely to have been made either to update these old-fashioned features or because the exemplar was physically disintegrating. Although it is possible to imagine a scenario in which a new *Beowulf* manuscript was made so that two readers could access the poem at the same time, it seems frankly unlikely: most classical Old English poetry does not seem to have had a wide readership, at least as measured by numbers of surviving manuscripts. It seems far

---

[7] E. A. Lowe, ed., *Codices Latini Antiquiores*, vol. II [Great Britain and Ireland] (Oxford: Clarendon Press, 1972) and Supplement (Oxford: Clarendon Press, 1971).

[8] Roberts, 'Lambeth Provenance'.

more likely to me to suppose that the existence of the new manuscript of *Beowulf* would have made the old one redundant. It was probably destroyed shortly thereafter, for who would prefer the old-fashioned (and possibly worn-out) book to the shiny new one?

It would be unfair of us, of course, to say that *we* would prefer to have the older version. But it is salutary, I think, to work through a thought experiment like this one if only to be reminded that our desire to possess an archetype of the surviving *Beowulf* manuscript seems to have very little bearing on what Anglo-Saxons might have thought. The unique survival of virtually all of the poems in the Nowell, Junius, Exeter, and Vercelli collections—as well as the unique survivals of *Waldere* and *Finnsburh*—would be most easily explained if the exemplars of these books (or the books themselves, in the case of material recycled in bindings) were destroyed early, rather than late.[9] In this context, it is striking to note that Lowe's photographic anthology of Latin manuscripts also shows a number of eighth-century or earlier manuscripts recycled as flyleaves or binding materials in England (or perhaps on the continent) as early as the ninth and tenth centuries (*CLA* 147, 150, 151, 176, 259), when the books in question were only a hundred or so years old. Even more relevant is the fact that the fullest version of the Old English *Solomon and Saturn* poem survives in Cambridge, Corpus Christi College manuscript 422, because it was apparently reused (as flyleaves or other binding material), perhaps soon after part B of the manuscript was copied around 1060, when, to judge by its own script, the *Solomon and Saturn* material was about a century old. Here, we have a clear example of the recycling of an older poetic manuscript as binding material, in circumstances that might obviously have also applied to other, similar books. In this case, the poem almost certainly survived the Anglo-Saxon period precisely because it had been recycled, rather than through any literary or bibliophilic merit. One wonders if it was recycled because it had recently been copied into a newer book itself, although no such newer book now survives. In fact, if both *Waldere* and *Finnsburh* did survive only as binding materials (as seems likely), they were probably already being used as such sometime between the tenth and thirteenth centuries.

---

[9] The Nowell, Junius, Exeter, and Vercelli books are the four most familiar repositories of Old English verse, representing about two-thirds of surviving classical Old English verse. All four books were made sometime between about 950 and 1020.

To put this issue into terms I have used above, virtually everything we know about book production in the Anglo-Saxon period suggests that the *Beowulf* scribes understood their role in the contemporary textual economy to be productive, rather than reproductive. Our desire to possess or access the *Beowulf* exemplar is itself a comment on our investment in 'the logic of the copy' inasmuch as it asserts a value in the exemplar that the 'copy' necessarily lacks. But the making of the *Beowulf* component of Cotton Vitellius A. xv was probably understood by these scribes as making a useful new book, rather than making a second example (a 'copy') of a still-useful book. When one makes a useful new book— especially if one is operating outside of the logic of the copy—it is perfectly sensible to suggest that the materials left over, the raw materials from which the book was made (even including exemplars) might well be seen as no longer being of value in themselves. Our tendency to conceptualize the very nature of scribal activity as reproductive—that is, as copying—is an interpretive anachronism that we must be careful to guard against. It is part and parcel of the logic of copying to recognize that the copy never equals the original: but if scribes (and Anglo-Saxons more generally) did not recognize the making of a new book as copying, it is perfectly plausible to suggest that they would see the new book as superior to the old, and that the old was thus disposable. One reason why so many classical Old English poems survive in only one manuscript may well be that their scribes did not think of them as copies, but as books—even if at the moment of their production they derived directly from another book.

It is very much worth noting here that similar claims about the central interpretive importance of the produced (as opposed to reproduced) manuscript have been made, especially in relation to Old English poetry, by scholars such as Carol Braun Pasternack, who writes the following in her own book's concluding paragraph: 'Since the manuscript texts, like oral productions, could be remade and recontextualized with any new production, the text as we have it represents the interests of its last maker and, we must presume, whoever financed its making, and a certain number of readers as well.'[10] I am struck, however, by Pasternack's linkage of such a perspective to the influence of orality: Pasternack's method

---

[10] Carol Braun Pasternack, *The Textuality of Old English Poetry*. Cambridge Studies in Anglo-Saxon England 13 (Cambridge: Cambridge University Press, 1995), p. 200.

allows her to draw this conclusion only in relation to Old English poetry, and it necessarily links this conclusion to the continuing influence of an oral and oral-formulaic tradition within the structures of what must surely be seen as a highly developed textual culture. But the key issues, it seems to me, are not at all limited to the realm of Old English poetry, and they can also be traced even in the non-linguistic material contents of books like recyclable vellum: the dynamic that underlies the perception of book-making as productive, rather than reproductive, is an aspect of early medieval textual, visual, and material culture, not a lingering inheritance from oral tradition. Such an understanding helps us understand the long lists of biblical and religious texts recycled in bindings already in the early middle ages, as described above: even the sacral content of such books was clearly not sufficient to prevent their recycling, and we must see that the usefulness of such books lay not merely in their texts, but also in their material.

Anglo-Saxon thinking about textual reproduction: Bede and Boniface

If the recycling of manuscripts in early medieval and later bindings helps us focus on the materiality, rather than the textuality, of Anglo-Saxon books, it nevertheless remains true that some books were duplicated with the purpose of reaching a broad, multiple readership: certainly, such duplication partakes of the logic of reproduction. Even so, I believe that a rereading of much Anglo-Saxon textual and visual culture will exemplify the ways in which the logic of production often predominated over the logic of reproduction during the period. To address the central issues, I will begin by contrasting two key examples from the eighth century, when the English literary tradition begins in earnest. The first case to be examined centres on Bede's *Historia ecclesiastica*, which was understood by its author as a text necessarily embedded within the ideology of textual reproduction: it was intended to be reproduced from a very early stage, and it was accompanied by a complex paratextuality that gave it shape and definition as a text. Yet Bede's great work, in the very process of its reproduction, was often treated by scribes in ways that individualized each manuscript; our contemporary focus on the stability of the textual content obscures the visual diversity of Bede manuscripts. Reading, here, to the degree that it allows us to move past or go beyond the visual component of these books, obscures the degree to which the model of textual reproduction in these books is complicated by their simultaneous investment in a paradigm of production.

Also situated in the eighth century, the Boniface correspondence may include the clearest and most explicit early English commentary on book-making activities. Yet nowhere among the surviving letters do Boniface or his correspondents ever clearly invoke the logic of the copy. As far as the Boniface correspondence seems to be concerned, the act of making a book was not a matter of copying or reproduction, but simply a matter of production. Likewise, when Boniface does express a preference for one physical manuscript over another, it has nothing to do with the logic of the copy: rather than preferring the exemplar to the copy for purely textual or media-oriented reasons, Boniface's preferences have to do only with purely visual matters of textual presentation. Boniface and Bede serve as bookends allowing us to glimpse the eighth-century perspective on a whole complex of issues and ideas.

The case of Bede's *Historia ecclesiastica*, finished, as Bede tells us, in 731, reminds us that from relatively early in the Anglo-Saxon period, scribal activity could indeed be understood as reproductive: in an authorial preface Bede address King Ceolwulf of Northumbria, saying 'Your Majesty has asked to see the *History of the English Church and Nation* which I have lately published. It was with pleasure, sire, that I submitted it for your perusal and criticism on a former occasion; and with pleasure I send it once again, for copying ["ad transcribendum"] and fuller study, as time may permit.'[11] Anticipating that Ceolwulf will not only study the manuscript but have it duplicated, Bede plainly recognizes that one manuscript of his book will not suffice and that publication entails the production of multiple copies of a work more or less simultaneously. To that degree, there is no doubt that Bede understands that books could be subject to reproductive copying, where the impetus of the individual scribal act is to produce *another book*, rather than to produce *a book*. In addition to the preface, the presence of Bede's own name on this work

---

[11] Translation by Bertram Colgrave and R. A. B. Mynors, eds. and trans., *Bede's Ecclesiastical History of the English People* (Oxford: Clarendon Press, 1969), p. 3; the Latin phrase is quoted from p. 2.

(given in the first sentence of the authorial preface); its title (which is usually reiterated in the headings that begin and end each book); and its carefully presented lists of chapter headings all serve as organizing and defining paratexts, and from very early indeed in the history of English letters, we see a clear association between the paratextual definition of a text and the intention to place a text into the realm of reproduction.

Yet the early history of Bede's great work, as far as we can reconstruct it, may well indicate that (at least as far as some details are concerned), scribes may have been responding to a somewhat different imperative, as can be seen in the record of the most famous portion of Bede's *Historia*, the story of Cædmon the cowherd and his miraculous gift of song-making. Strikingly, two of the earliest and best manuscripts of the *Historia ecclesiastica* include Old English versions of *Cædmon's Hymn*, the Moore manuscript having the *Hymn* entered at the end of the book as a whole, while the St Petersburg manuscript has the *Hymn* entered at the bottom margin of the relevant page of book iv, chapter 24.[12] For these early scribes, supplementing Bede's Latin book was apparently both desirable and appropriate. Nor did these scribes' apparent proximity to Bede's own scriptorium hinder their willingness to modify his text, at least to this extent.

It is important to note that other eighth-century versions of the *Historia*, such as Kassel, Landesbibliothek 4° MS. theol. 2, do not include *Cædmon's Hymn* at all. We might go further in noting textual variations: Colgrave and Mynors, in their edition, note that two main textual traditions of the *Historia* survive, one lacking the story of 'A miracle of St Oswald (iv. 14)' which is preserved in the other.[13] This difference may ultimately derive from revision on Bede's part, just as his comments to Ceolwulf imply that more than one version of the work as a whole might well have been both authored and authorized. Some manuscripts preserve an added annalistic contribution, the *Continuatio Bedae*, extending beyond Bede's death.[14]

The very early Moore and St Petersburg manuscripts also differ from one another in that the Moore manuscript is characterized by 'the

---

[12] The Moore manuscript is Cambridge, Cambridge University Library, KK. 5. 16; the St Petersburg Bede manuscript is Saint Petersburg, National Library of Russia, lat. Q. v. I. 18.

[13] Colgrave and Mynors, eds. and trans., *Bede's Ecclesiastical History*, p. xli.

[14] Colgrave and Mynors, eds. and trans., *Bede's Ecclesiastical History*, pp. lxvii–lxix.

absence of ornament', while the St Petersburg manuscript is 'a very hand-some volume with fine ornament'.[15] One can, and should, say more about the differences between these two early books: the St Petersburg manu-script begins chapter 1 of book i with an eleven-line initial B, with the rest of the letters of 'Britannia' laid out in a kind of mosaic pattern in three tiers covering the same eleven lines.[16] The page (and the book as a whole) is laid out in two columns, and even a quick glance through the facsimile reveals a number of layout choices designed to ease readers' route through the text: the lists of chapter headings are presented in a tabular format; capital letters are used for headings; uncials are often used for colophons or the dating clauses of quoted letters. Words are generally separated from one another. These matters of *ordinatio* in the arrangement of the page and of the book complement the complex para-textuality which structures Bede's great history, with its prefaces, books, chapters, lists of chapter headings, and title. The degree to which matters of *ordinatio* so often involve paratexts suggests an effective coordination between paratextual and medial definitions of this text.

By comparison, the *ordinatio* of the Moore manuscript is a far less effective match for Bede's work. The analogous page of this book, folio 3r, shows the end of the list of chapter headings, the *explicit* and *incipit* rubrics, and the opening words of the first chapter.[17] The list of chapter heads is written continuously, instead of in tabular format, and this manuscript uses a single-column layout, exhibits a distinct lack of spac-ing between the words, and generally avoids any white space on the page; such practices make for a very different visual effect from that achieved by the St Petersburg manuscript. The uneven bottom margin on this particular page is clearly an original feature of the book, leading to an abbreviated line at the bottom of the page. The Moore manuscript does use rubrication for the chapter numbers and *explicit/incipit* here (as well as making some use of uncials, though more sparingly than St Peters-burg). The relative lack of spacing and differentiation between all levels

[15] Colgrave and Mynors, eds. and trans., *Bede's Ecclesiastical History*, pp. xliii–xliv.

[16] This detail and other visual details from this manuscript are visible in O. Arngart, ed., *The Leningrad Bede*, EEMF 2 (Copenhagen: Rosenkilde and Bagger, 1952), fo. 3v. The same page is, at the time of this writing, also shown on the St Petersburg Bede's Wikipedia page in a coloured image which is identified as being in the public domain.

[17] Visual details of the Moore manuscript can be seen in Peter Hunter Blair, ed., *The Moore Bede*, EEMF 9 (Copenhagen: Rosenkilde and Bagger, 1959).

of the text (words, sections, books), like the single-column layout, literally makes the Moore manuscript comparatively difficult to read, reminding us again that legibility and visual effects do not always operate well together. The Moore manuscript is written to make efficient use of the vellum that is available; the physical material of the book appears to constrain the scribe in important ways. This scribe, even while reproducing Bede's text, exemplifies an attitude that shows a clear prioritization of the book as a unique produced object or artefact. The extensive visual differences between these two early manuscripts remind us that the visible components of these books should not be passed over too quickly.

Indeed, while in their early history the manuscripts of this important Latin work show a fairly high degree of uniformity in the Latin text itself (give or take the presence or absence of Oswald's miracle or *Cædmon's Hymn*), they often differ extensively in other features. Even in the context of a work whose words (considered as legible, rather than visible) remained fairly stable across a spectrum of manuscripts, these kinds of textual and visual differences remind us that each of the eighth-century copies of Bede's greatest work remains unique and distinct from the others. Each scribe or team of scribes was clearly making decisions on the basis of the book he, she, or they wanted to produce: each book was a unique production, even as it remained an example of Bede's *Historia*. The general (but far from complete, even in the eighth-century copies) stability of their textual component is a remarkable feature of the production of these early books, but it is not clear that textual stability in itself is indicative of an attitude that scribal work is essentially reproductive in nature—unless we focus on the legible stability of the surviving manuscript texts at the expense of their visible diversity. To put it in other terms, even when eighth-century scribes were engaged in making new and multiple copies of Bede's *Historia*, their choices and range of action were, to judge by the surviving examples, at least partially consonant with a perspective that saw each resulting physical book as a unique production.

This understanding will help us think through other Anglo-Saxon textual productions as well. For example, we generally understand the production of sacred texts like the Christian gospels or the psalms as necessitating a high degree of textual accuracy, and it is tempting for us to assume or conclude that Anglo-Saxon scribes therefore understood and operated through the paradigm of copying, in which their role was duplicative and reproductive, rather than productive. The sheer number of surviving manuscripts of both the gospels and the psalms might encourage us to see things in just these terms. Yet these manuscripts, too, almost always feature up-to-date scripts, so far as we can tell: textual accuracy and fidelity did not extend to the visible, as opposed to legible, portions of books.[18] It may well be worth noting once again how often biblical or liturgical manuscripts seem to have been recycled as binding fragments, even in the Anglo-Saxon period itself. Unless there was a special reason to preserve an old gospel book (such as elaborate decoration or association with an important personage), it was apparently considered expendable, and thus we might reasonably conclude that the act of making a gospel book was not always aimed at multiplying the text, but about producing a useful, up-to-date, and readable book. Richly illuminated gospel manuscripts like the Books of Durrow and Kells and the Lindisfarne Gospels are each fine examples, of course, of singular, even unique, productions; their very survival complements the evidence of the recycling of other eighth-century gospel books to suggest the paradigm of production dominated the making of books even as sacred as the gospels.[19] There can be no doubt that manuscripts often served as exemplars for other manuscripts, whether we are thinking of gospel books, Bede's *Historia*, or even *Beowulf*. But the use of books as exemplars in itself is clearly not determinative of a paradigmatic view of book-making as reproductive.

Bede's Anglo-Saxon contemporary, Boniface, offers us a different perspective, partly because he expresses his clearest views on book-making and book duplication not in relation to his own works, but rather in a remarkable series of letters and correspondence. Indeed, one of the most

[18] An exception to the general rule of updating scripts can be seen in the early eighth-century bibles produced at Ceolfrith's Wearmouth/Jarrow. As summarized by Michelle P. Brown, 'The Triumph of the Codex: The Manuscript Book Before 1100', in Simon Eliot and Jonathan Rose, eds., *A Companion to the History of the Book* (Oxford: Blackwell, 2007), pp. 179–93, at p. 184, the Codex Amiatinus 'was taken by Abbot Ceolfrith as a present to the Pope in 716 and subsequently considered the work of Italo-Byzantine, rather than English craftsmen.... Yet it was no antiquarian facsimile but a dynamic feat of editorial scholarship, probably led by Bede.' Amiatinus is Florence, Bibl. Medicea-Laurenziana, MS Amiatino 1.

[19] The Book of Durrow is Dublin, Trinity College Library, A. 4. 5. (57); The Book of Kells is Dublin, Trinity College Library, A. 1. (58); the Lindisfarne Gospels manuscript is London, British Library, Cotton Nero D. iv.

consistent recurring features of the Boniface correspondence is his series of requests for particular books, the thanks he gives for receiving them, and his comments on his own transmission of texts (see letters 15, 27, 30, 33, 34, 35, 63, 75, 76, 77, and 91).[20] In three cases, Boniface asks his correspondents for access to the writings of his recently deceased Northumbrian contemporary, Bede (letters 75, 76, and 91). In a letter addressed to Abbot Hwætberht of Wearmouth in about 747, Boniface writes 'we beg you to be so kind as to copy and send us some of the treatises of that keenest investigator of the Scriptures, the monk Bede, who, we have learned, shone forth among you of late as a lantern of the Church.'[21] Boniface's original Latin, however, uses only the participle 'conscripta' ('gathered in writing') where Emerton translates 'copy.'[22] At the risk of quibbling over a translation, it seems important to note that the association of book-making with *copia*, plentifulness, does not seem to have appeared until some hundreds of years later; in Boniface's eighth-century letters, he asks his correspondents to send him books or to write them for him, but he does not ask them to engage in copying.

Further, it is important to note the ways in which the Boniface correspondence conceptualizes the processes of textual making and transmission. In the first relevant letter, Boniface's correspondent Bugga sends her regrets for having been unable to send him the 'passiones martyrum' ('passions of the martyrs') that he had requested.[23] When she is able, she will do so, she suggests ('dum valeam, faciam'), though her phrasing seems ambiguously to suggest either that when she can find such a book she will send it, or that she will, indeed, make the book ('faciam') when she is able.[24] In letter 27, Boniface explicitly notes that he has been unable to finish writing some 'sentences' ('sententiarum') that Bugga had asked him for.[25] In letter 34, Boniface asks a former pupil to send him any books in his library that might be of use, but whether Duddo is expected to send existing examples or newly written versions is not clear. Certainly, in letter 63, Boniface has a specific book in mind,

---

[20] Michael Tangl, ed., *Die Briefe des Heiligen Bonifatius und Lullus*, 2nd edition (Berlin: Weidmannische Verlagsbuchhandlung, 1955).

[21] Ephraim Emerton, trans., *The Letters of Saint Boniface*, with a new introduction and bibliography by Thomas F. X. Noble (New York: Columbia University Press, 2000), p. 112.

[22] Tangl, ed., *Die Briefe des Heiligen Bonifatius und Lullus*, p. 159.

[23] Tangl, ed., *Die Briefe des Heiligen Bonifatius und Lullus*, p. 27.

[24] Tangl, ed., *Die Briefe des Heiligen Bonifatius und Lullus*, p. 27.

[25] Tangl, ed., *Die Briefe des Heiligen Bonifatius und Lullus*, p. 48.

one that is not a newly made duplicate: 'send me the book of the Prophets which Abbot Winbert of reverend memory, my former teacher, left when he passed from this life to the Lord.... [W]ith my fading sight I cannot read well writing which is small and filled with abbreviations. I am asking for this book because it is copied clearly, with all letters distinctly written out.'[26] In some of these cases, newly made books seem to be being exchanged, but that need not necessarily be the case in general. Boniface's desire for what we would call the original, here, has nothing to do with textual integrity, and everything to do with visible legibility: nowhere in Boniface's letters does he distinguish between an 'original' and a 'copy' in such a way as to imply a hierarchy of value that invokes the 'logic of the copy'.

In letter 33, Boniface asks Archbishop Nothhelm for an 'exemplar' of the correspondence between Augustine and Gregory; the same word ('exemplaria') is again used in relation to some further letters of Gregory in letter 75.[27] Here, Boniface's Latin seems almost directly to contrast with our own terminology, as we tend to see exemplars as originals, rather than copies. But Boniface seems to use the word simply to mean 'example', or possibly 'transcript', and the very ambiguity of the term exposes the unimportance of drawing a clear distinction between what we would identify as copy and exemplar throughout Boniface's letters. What Boniface's correspondence teaches us here is that our concerns, especially as they articulate a hierarchical relationship of value between original and copy, do not map very well at all onto his apparent concerns.

One could hardly imagine two English figures in the early and middle eighth century who were more highly literate and textually oriented than Bede and Boniface. And Bede certainly understands how using paratexts to give his great work an identity (centred on its localization in time and space as well as its proper boundaries) is a useful strategy in the making and marketing of a book that will be duplicated and reproduced widely. Yet in the activities of contemporary scribes, including Boniface and his correspondents as well as the Moore and St Petersburg scribes, we see the power of a perspective on book-making that remains invested in the ideology of production, rather than reproduction. Our habitual or

---

[26] Emerton, trans., *The Letters of Saint Boniface*, p. 94.
[27] Tangl, ed., *Die Briefe des Heiligen Bonifatius und Lullus*, p. 57 and p. 158.

conventional focus on Bede's text, as text, urges us to recognize only the reproductive dynamic at work, but eighth-century books often owed as much or more to their status as productions—which we must see, as well as read.

Alfred and after

A century and more later, and focused on Old English rather than Latin texts, the Alfredian programme of translation and book dissemination at the end of the ninth century provides confirmation that the multiplication of 'copies' of a book in this period still had much to share with an ideology that conceptualized each manuscript of a book as a unique production. The most familiar example is Oxford, Bodleian Library, Hatton 20, the copy of Alfred's *Pastoral Care* translation that was sent to Bishop Wærferth of Worcester at the time of publication. Let me restate that a bit more clearly: this book containing Alfred's *Pastoral Care* is not some mere generic 'copy': it has been specifically personalized for a particular recipient. The individuation of this manuscript involved not only the addition of a prose letter or preface naming the recipient explicitly, but also a verse preface and a verse epilogue. Other original copies seem at least sometimes to have had similar personalizing letters, and while the verse preface is preserved in four manuscripts, the verse epilogue survives in only two, which suggests the possibility that the inclusion of this epilogue was variable or optional from the very beginning.[28]

Like Bede's Preface to the *Historia ecclesiastica*, Alfred's prose preface identifies himself as author, specifies a recipient (Wærferth, in the case of Hatton 20), and gives the translation a title: 'on Læden *Pastoralis*, ond on Englisc "Hierdebōc"' ('in Latin *Pastoralis* and in English *Hierdeboc*').[29] Prose or verse prefaces also accompany other books in Alfred's programme: *Boethius*, *The Laws of Alfred and Ine*, Augustine's *Soliloquies*, and Wærferth's translation of *Gregory's Dialogues*; other paratextual support aids in the textual definition of *Orosius* (a title is given in the Cotton

---

[28] The details of the relevant manuscripts are given in Krapp and Dobbie, eds., *The Anglo-Saxon Minor Poems*, ASPR vol. 6, pp. cxiii–cxv.

[29] I cite the Preface from the convenient student edition in Bruce Mitchell and Fred C. Robinson, *A Guide to Old English*, 7th edition (Oxford: Blackwell, 2007), pp. 216–19. The quoted passage falls on p. 219; the translation is my own.

manuscript; both manuscripts include a list of chapter headings).[30] Once again, the association between an understanding of the text as defined and delimited by paratext and an understanding that a text will be multi-plied and reproduced seems notable.

Interestingly, however, Alfred's prose preface to the *Pastoral Care* gives us remarkable insight into his own apparent perspective on the unique value of individual books, as at least partially distinct from the texts they contain. Thinking back on a time before he himself had taken the throne in 871, Alfred recalled how he had seen, 'ær ðæm ðe hit eall forhergod wære ond forbærned, hū ðā ciricean giond eall Angelcynn stōdon māðma ond bōca gefylda' ('before it was all harried and burned, how the churches all around England stood filled with treasures and books').[31] This imaginative equation between treasures and books is picked up later on, when Alfred notes that he is attaching an *æstel* (val-ued by Alfred at fifty mancusses, or 1,500 silver pence) to each copy of the book, with the request that books and *æstels* not be separated from one another. The well-known Alfred Jewel, of course, has long been understood as likely to have been one of these treasures, and while the legible portions of the relevant books may have been very similar indeed, the presence of the *æstels* and the prefaces or letters attached to each individual book appears to make each of Alfred's copies unique. Each book was a unique treasure, in Alfred's terms, and it is tempting to sus-pect that one purpose the *æstels* served was specifically to help make each physical book in the translation programme materially and visibly distinct from the others.

What this Alfredian example suggests, then, is that while it was cer-tain that Alfred knew that books could be multiplied (he even imag-ines that Wærferth might lend out Hatton 20 as an exemplar to be reproduced, just as Bede assumes Ceolfrith might have the *Historia* duplicated), that knowledge alone did not suffice to change the whole

---

[30] The verse prefaces to *Boethius* and Wærferth's translation of *Gregory's Dialogues* can be found in Krapp, ed., *The Paris Psalter and the Meters of Boethius*, ASPR vol. 5, p. 153 and *The Anglo-Saxon Minor Poems*, ASPR vol. 6, pp. 112–13; the preface to the *Laws* is probably most easily accessible in facsimile in Robin Flower and Hugh Smith, *The Parker Chronicle and Laws*, EETS o.s. 208 (Oxford: EETS, 1941 for 1937), fos. 36r–39v; for the *Soliloquies*, see Thomas A. Carnicelli, ed., *King Alfred's Version of St. Augustine's Soliloquies* (Cambridge, MA: Harvard University Press, 1969); for *Orosius*, see Janet Bately, ed., *The Old English Orosius*, EETS s.s. 6 (Oxford: EETS, 1980).

[31] Mitchell and Robinson, *Guide*, pp. 271–8.

paradigm of book production into a paradigm of reproduction, even in his own thinking. Another useful example to consider involves the manuscripts of *The Anglo-Saxon Chronicle*, which span from around the year 900 into the middle of the twelfth century.[32] From an early stage indeed, the *Chronicle*'s potential for supplementation by additional annals might make it seem exceptional in the way in which each manuscript more or less naturally becomes a unique production, rather than a reproduction. But the uniqueness of each *Chronicle* manuscript manifests itself in another manner as well, in the ways in which the books containing the *Chronicle* did or did not include other texts: *The West Saxon Regnal Table* was associated with manuscripts A, B, and G (which was, in part, a duplicate of A made in the first quarter of the eleventh century); in the tenth century, *The Laws of Alfred and Ine* were added to A; *Orosius*, *The Menologium*, and *Maxims II* were associated with the C Chronicle tradition, perhaps as early as the late tenth century; *The Old English Bede* was associated with the destroyed G version. Only the latest versions (D, E, and F) are truly stand-alone *Chronicle* manuscripts—and they all begin with a descriptive geographical preface derived from Bede.

From our perspective, *The Anglo-Saxon Chronicle* is a text, at some level, but as far as Anglo-Saxon book-makers were concerned, each of these books was individual and unique, and not understood or defined as a duplicate or 'copy' of some authoritative exemplar or original. We can think about each *Chronicle* manuscript as a 'copy' of a particular stage of the overall textual development of the whole (and for our purposes it is sometimes useful to do so), but there is a crucial sense in which such a perspective privileges the legible over the material and the visible. As physical books, the *Chronicle* manuscripts are widely variable in size and shape, as well as in what other works accompany the *Chronicle*: each version of the *Chronicle* is a part of a unique book produced at a particular moment in time. Not only does the textual uniqueness of each *Chronicle* manuscript attest to a conceptual paradigm of book production, but the physical distinctiveness of each version as a compiled or composed book gives precisely the same impression.

he *Chronicle* and its manuscripts and their textual associations, see Thomas A. *Textual Histories: Readings in the* Anglo-Saxon Chronicle (Toronto: University Press, 2001).

It is useful to think through the example of *The Anglo-Saxon Chronicle* from another perspective, however. As a text the *Chronicle* is very likely to have been promoted or begun in Alfred's literary programme, but it never had a definitively Alfredian preface. Lacking an explicit paratextual apparatus, the *Chronicle* travelled without a named or specified author, without a specified local or historical context, and without a title. Lacking those key elements which would have served to identify the *Chronicle* as a bounded and defined text, manuscripts of the *Chronicle* quickly exceeded any such boundaries, with a variety of textual accretions (as listed above), revisions (such as the Northern Recension), and numerous additional annals and continuations. One of the most remarkable features of the *Chronicle* is its extensive if discontinuous history of additions, extending in one case to the middle of the twelfth century; this adaptability and extensibility was a consequence of its very lack of definition as a bounded and historically situated text. To the degree that *Chronicle* manuscripts did not feature a paratextual apparatus to indicate author, title, and the rest, the *Chronicle* operated as a non-medial, non-text production, with ill-defined boundaries and no necessary or consistent content or identity. The very openness of the *Chronicle* format, so marvellously employed by generations of chroniclers, was founded upon its manuscript presentation without a paratextual apparatus. Rather than operating in the realm of reproduction, from the very beginning, manuscripts of the *Chronicle* were always unique productions, leading to the diversity we see in them today. Part of what makes the *Chronicle* valuable as a continuing historical record was enabled by its very lack of textual definition, its lack of bounding and localization as determined by an author and historical context.

As with the example of Bede, we see again here that even within a literary scene which explicitly used paratextual apparatus as a means of defining and situating texts in relation to an active programme of textual reproduction, Anglo-Saxon books were not entirely determined by the ideology of reproduction. The individualization of particular books as well the supplementation of the *Chronicle* manuscripts remind us of the power of the perception of each physical book as a unique, local production. It is remarkable, and very likely significant, that more manuscripts of *The Anglo-Saxon Chronicle* survive than any of the works explicitly associated with Alfred's translation programme. An investment in the logic of reproduction and textual definition was apparently no guarantee that a work would in fact be widely disseminated, and the *Chronicle*'s utility as a series of unique productions led to a greater number of produced *Chronicle* manuscripts that survive than for any of Alfred's intended reproductions.

The rood poems in the tenth century

The ways in which the books containing *The Anglo-Saxon Chronicle* differ—in their versions of the *Chronicle*; in their associated works; and in their differing shapes, sizes, scripts, and presentation—can stand as emblematic of the working of a textual culture that sees textual making as productive rather than reproductive. It is useful, however, to recognize the way in which such a perspective applies in other areas of visual culture as well. Specifically, my discussion of the *Chronicle* can usefully be supplemented by a consideration of the Vercelli version of *The Dream of the Rood* in comparison with the poems and prose material found on the Ruthwell and Brussels crosses. The poem in each case is different; each one is associated with quite different sets of other written or visual material; and each is preserved in a unique physical and visual environment, quite different from the others.

The nature of the relationship between the Vercelli poem and the Ruthwell stone cross is a question under more or less constant debate in Anglo-Saxon studies; the Brussels Cross, perhaps because of its textual brevity, is less rarely considered in equal detail, though it certainly ought to be. All three deserve at least brief description here, if only to clarify what is at stake for our understanding of Anglo-Saxon visual and textual culture.

I will begin with *The Dream of the Rood*, a poem of 156 lines, preserved in the Vercelli manuscript, a grand collection of Old English prose homilies and religious verse surviving in Vercelli, although likely written in Canterbury in the second half of the tenth century.[33] Like the other large collections containing Old English verse, the poems in the Vercelli book are generally anonymous, and their dates of composition remain matters of debate,

---

[33] For the poem, see Krapp, ed., *The Vercelli Book*, ASPR vol. 3, pp. 6–65; for the localization of the manuscript, see Donald Scragg, ed., *The Vercelli Homilies*, EETS o.s. 300 (Oxford: EETS, 1992), pp. lxxiv–lxxix.

although it is likely that most of the poems in the Vercelli book date from the late ninth century or earlier. Thus, the Vercelli book is likely to include poems a century or more old at the time of its writing, and these poems may well have derived from exemplars old enough to need updating or replacing. In its remarkable presentation of a dreamer who receives a vision of the cross, the poem deserves the high regard which modern critics give it.

The Ruthwell Cross poem, contrastingly, consists of only fourteen fragmentary lines (some of which are unpaired half-lines), carved in runes upon the margins of a pair of vine scrolls on the narrow sides of the Ruthwell Cross, a sandstone shaft somewhat over five metres tall.[34] The front and back of the Cross have carvings of biblical scenes with accompanying Latin texts, although some runes are also used on the headpiece of the Cross. The runes of the poem are practically unreadable, at least in their layout in short lines of three to five runes, and their comparatively small size may add to the difficulty of reading the poem. Notably, there is no dreamer figure implied in this poem; the speaking voice belongs to the biblical cross. The date of the Ruthwell Cross is usually placed in the eighth century; the date at which the poem's runes were carved cannot be before the rest of the cross, but it may well be a good deal later, perhaps even as late as the Vercelli book itself, and scholars have debated the point extensively, and often quite vehemently.

The Brussels Cross takes the form of a wooden reliquary, apparently designed to hold a piece of the true cross and made in the late tenth or early eleventh century.[35] A silver band runs around the periphery of this cross; the poetic text is inscribed in capital letters upon this band. Here we have only two poetic lines (corresponding somewhat roughly to Vercelli lines 44 and 48), along with a prose commissioner's inscription.[36] Another surface of the cross has the maker's inscription, 'Drahmal me worhte' ('Drahmal made me'). Again, there is no dreamer figure, and if the reliquary was designed to hold a fragment of the true cross, the speaking voice would be especially apposite. Notably, the poem is almost impossible to read unless one holds the reliquary in one's hands and

---

[34] Krapp and Dobbie, eds., *The Anglo-Saxon Minor Poems*, ASPR vol. 6, pp. 114–15.

[35] Krapp and Dobbie, eds., *The Anglo-Saxon Minor Poems*, ASPR vol. 6, p. 115.

[36] The formal analogues to the prose portion of the Brussels Cross are from the inscriptional tradition, rather than the manuscript tradition. In that sense, the commissioners' component of the Brussels inscription does not really function as an authorial paratext, and it certainly is not implicated in issues of reproduction.

turns it to see the various strips of silver banding, although photographs can be used to juxtapose the relevant parts of the inscription onto a single page.

Whatever else we say about *The Dream of the Rood* as a poem to be considered alongside the poems on the Ruthwell and Brussels crosses, it is certain that none of these items can be seen as a 'copy' of any of the others. Executed at different lengths, in different media (vellum manuscript, stone cross, silver bands), in different scripts (Old English bookhand, runes, inscriptional capitals) and presumably at different locations (perhaps Canterbury?; Ruthwell; Wessex?), each of these poems must be seen as a unique, individual, and local production, made for a local audience. As tempting as it is to see these poems as evidence for widespread knowledge of a particular text, which we might imagine as a poem very like *The Dream of the Rood*, I am not at all sure that the evidence supports such a conclusion. Even our contemporary habit of reading these items alongside one another is probably anachronistic. That is, as comfortable as it is to claim (with Swanton) that the Ruthwell Cross poem 'has all the appearance of reference to or quotation from some familiar text', it is not really possible to show that readers would be familiar with the source of the quoted material.[37] Indeed, any claim of the poem's popularity or widespread diffusion can be argued solely on the survival of the Vercelli book and the two crosses, which explicitly ignores the manifest differences among the poems. That there is a relationship among the three poems seems indisputable, but we must take care about whether we see that relationship as dominated by reproduction or not. If we are willing to see these poems as characterized instead by production, the manifest differences between them simply express their separate identities as productions based in separate historically situated times and places.

Two points must be made clearly here. First, the Ruthwell verses serve as a quotation only if readers recognize their source, or at least are expected to do so. As discussed in the Introduction above, it is in the nature of quotation to operate through synecdoche, the quoted part calling up or standing in for the absent whole in some fashion. To imagine or understand the Ruthwell verses as a quotation demands that we accept the notion that there is a whole text from which they derive. In short,

---

[37] Michael Swanton, ed., *The Dream of the Rood*, new edition (Exeter: University of Exeter Press, 1996), p. 41.

even raising the issue of whether the Ruthwell (or Brussels) verses are quoted implicitly identifies them as texts, in the sense that they are literally conceptualized as imperfect or incomplete representations of a whole which nevertheless exists somewhere, even if only in some readers' minds. We see again that the very notion of a quotation invokes the logic of the copy. Our recognition of a relationship among these texts cannot be used to show that any one of them was a text subject to reproduction, as that is the very question at issue.

The second necessary point is a related one: if these verses are quotations, just what whole would they call up in readers' minds? Swanton's phrase, 'some familiar text', glosses over this difficulty with remarkable smoothness, and most of Swanton's readers presumably imagine that the familiar text that was called to Anglo-Saxon minds would be the same as the familiar text that is called to their minds: the Vercelli *Dream*, which is very familiar indeed to modern medievalists. But the very uniqueness and artefactuality of the Brussels and Ruthwell crosses remind us that the Vercelli *Dream* could be just as much a unique production: an expansion, abbreviation, or combination of some previously existing poetic materials. Our habitual practice of tracing source-relations across or among these three poems urges us not to multiply unknowns, and to locate the 'source' for verses or words from the cross poems in the Vercelli *Dream*—but doing so also casts all three into the paradigmatic world of texts, because it is the logic of the copy that allows the tracing of sources and borrowings. Again, these are the consequences of thinking of the Ruthwell or Brussels verses as quotations. It is far more effective, I believe, to recognize all three poems as unique, non-medial, non-text artefacts or productions, cobbled together for unique local purposes, although making use of some of the same raw materials.

Obviously, what is at stake here is the very nature of *The Dream of the Rood* as a 'text'. Presented in the Vercelli manuscript without even the most basic paratextual apparatus, the Vercelli *Dream*, like virtually all classical Old English verse, has a remarkably ill-defined identity as a 'text'. The lack of textual definition as modulated by paratextual apparatus gives what we textualize as '*The Dream*' a lack of boundary definition that opens it (or its raw materials) up for being remade into new productions, just as we saw with the *Chronicle*.

In this lack of paratextual materials, *The Dream* is typical of classical Old English poetry, which generally survives in context with virtually no paratextual apparatus at all: with only a handful of exceptions, Old English poems have no titles; no external ascriptions of authorship; no prefaces; no glossing; no commentary; no scribal, authorial, or publisher's commentary; and (usually) nothing else, either. If we understand paratextual apparatus as part of what helps us define a text, we must acknowledge that in their original contexts Old English poems must even have an unclear status as texts, a circumstance that is spectacularly confirmed by modern critical uncertainty about textual boundaries in relation to Old English poems: should we read *Christ I*, *Christ II*, and *Christ III* as one poem or three?[38] *Riddles* 1–3? Are *Guthlac A* and *Guthlac B* one poem or two? Does the prose *Solomon and Saturn* make all of the *Solomon and Saturn* material into a prosimetrum, or should we see it as two poems and a prose composition? Does the sequential numbering of sections in Liber I of the Junius manuscript mean that *Genesis A*, *Genesis B*, *Exodus*, and *Daniel* make up one long poem? Or, perhaps even more provocatively, is the Cynewulfian signature passage which follows the 'finit' of *Elene* text or paratext? In all of these cases, the almost complete lack of paratextual cues about the nature or boundaries of Old English verse texts leaves modern readers in a state of uncertainty, and our modern titles for all these works (so very useful to the current discussion!) serve explicitly to express the contemporary notion that a text is incomplete and undefined without at least the minimal paratext of a title. Debates about whether *Christ I* should be labelled '*Christ I*', 'the first part of *Christ*', or '*The Advent Lyrics*' (a title that suggests we may not be dealing with one poem, but several) reveal even more clearly our need to understand the nature of the text through a paratextual title. The modern critical consensus about textual boundaries in relation to these works, I would point out, is merely a convenient fiction, and a function of the manuscripts' failure or refusal to do the work of textual definition in the first place. But since these manuscript items are made into texts (according to the paratextual definition, at least) in the act of assigning them modern titles, line numbering, and the like, it is apparent that in their manuscript context, they operate outside of the paratextual definition of text entirely. The challenges posed by these items in their

---

[38] The Old English poems discussed in this paragraph and the following may all be found in the relevant volumes of Krapp and Dobbie, eds., *The Anglo-Saxon Poetic Records*.

manuscript contexts are quite different in kind from the interpretational challenges posed by texts, and our habit of making them into texts before we even begin the work of interpretation is a matter of convenience that does violence to their original materiality.

Similarly, when classical Old English poems do show reliance on identical source material, the logic of the copy does not really apply. *Daniel* (764 lines) and *Azarias* (191 lines) closely parallel each other for a number of lines (around 75), but they are clearly two very different compositions, with different sizes and purposes. Likewise, the Vercelli *Soul and Body I* is incomplete, ending in the middle of line 166, while the Exeter *Soul and Body II* appears to be complete at 121 lines; the Vercelli version closely parallels the Exeter poem, but extends well beyond it. The persistent suggestion that Cynewulf may have reworked earlier compositions and added his name in signature passages could also be understood as resulting from a lack of definition of his poetic source material as 'texts'.[39] To put it in other terms, a 'text', as an entity implicitly subject to reproduction, necessarily always has well-defined boundaries that must be respected in the process of reproduction, and those boundaries are (at least implicitly) associated with a title and the name or intention of an author. Certainly, in the *Daniel/Azarias* and *Soul and Body* examples, there is no clear evidence of any scribe's or poet's intention to respect textual boundaries in the process of composition or writing. Just as modern scholars cannot always be certain about textual boundaries in relation to Old English verse, Anglo-Saxons appear to have often felt unconstrained by a respect for textual boundaries in relation to the manuscript production of classical Old English poems. The principle of textual fidelity that the logic of the copy both demands and undermines—the copy is always a (mis)representation of the original—does not seem to have applied for much classical Old English poetry, or indeed for much Anglo-Saxon material in general.

To return, then, to the case of *The Dream of the Rood*, there is no clear reason why we should suspect that those responsible for the Brussels and Ruthwell poems ever expected that they would be copied or recopied, just as the radically differing lengths of all three related items express a lack of agreement on boundaries. Likewise, there is literally no evidence

---

[39] See Daniel Donoghue, *Style in Old English Poetry: The Test of the Auxiliary* (New Haven: Yale University Press, 1987), pp. 115–16.

for suspecting that readers were expected to recognize either cross poem as a quotation from a longer work: that becomes possible for us only when we reproduce these items and literally make them into texts. As far as we can see, the poems on these objects were not, indeed, produced with reproduction in mind, in either direction. In their original contexts, they are artefacts or productions, not texts, in the sense that texts always are invested in reproduction, at one level or another. The inevitable conclusion is that the Vercelli *Dream* very probably has the same status: there is no clear evidence that it was ever intended to be reproduced, nor that it was produced via an attempt to replicate or represent an original. Nor can we claim with any confidence that the Vercelli *Dream* even shares its boundary points with any prior exemplar. It seems very likely to me that this poem was produced with the intention to make a poem, not to copy one, for it to be a poem, not to represent one. It was probably intended to be as autonomous as either the Ruthwell or Brussels poem: not a text but an artefact. We are unlikely to think of the activities of the Ruthwell or Brussels designers as mere copying, but because the Vercelli manuscript is a book, we fall too easily into a habit of conceptualizing the Vercelli scribe as a copyist.

The crosses have at least one more lesson for us, however. The notion of a 'text' as a well-defined and bounded object is explicitly invoked in the distinction between text and paratext: text is central, and generally surrounded (physically, figuratively, or both) by paratext, which serves to define a text's boundaries or extent, to historicize it, and to associate it with an author or authority figure, if only by invoking an original that can serve as a locus of authority lying behind imperfect material copies. On both the Ruthwell and Brussels crosses, the Old English poetic material is explicitly marginal: located in the margins of the narrow sides of the cross shaft at Ruthwell, or inscribed on the encircling silver bands of the Brussels reliquary. In their marginality, the poems operate more like paratexts, helping to define the crosses themselves as central, than like central texts accompanied by paratext. The marginality of both poems is thus very probably to be associated with their status as artefacts or productions, one more aspect of the way in which these poems lie outside the economy of reproduction that is essential to 'textual' definition and identity.

In the end, when we read, print, and textualize these cross poems in such a way as to minimize the importance of seeing them and what they surround, we actually invert the visual/textual hierarchies explicit in these artefacts: seeing these artefacts surely demands the construal of the letters or runes, but we should not 'read' them as texts. In the case of the Ruthwell Cross in particular, the runic script and the challenging short-line layout and lack of word spacing are not mere hurdles lying between us and some ideal text they obscure: the runes and layout are essential components of this artefactual object. If we attempt to read *through* such visual details to an underlying, purely linguistic 'work', we assume or assert that the Ruthwell poem is a media-textual object, and its visible form is a mere curiosity or context. Such *reading through* is the mode of reading appropriate for texts and textual media, but it is not at all appropriate for artefacts or productions.

We need a new way of seeing: editorial strategies that re-present the runes and characters on these crosses via typography, transliteration, relineation, and so forth explicitly cast these items into the realm of copies or texts, in which their visual, visible form is treated as a meaningless accidental phenomenon, a barrier between us and the poems that can be ignored or even replaced without significant loss. To the degree that modern scholars of these items rely on printed, transliterated, or even photographic representations, we run the risk of also treating the originals as medial in such a fashion as to indicate that the real objects of our interest are the immaterial (linguistic) works which the physical objects and texts both grant access to and obscure. But what the Ruthwell and Brussels crosses teach us most clearly is that artefactual productions are not medial at all. Textual media always involve the logic of the copy and thus are explicitly medial; artefactual productions confront viewers with things in themselves, not some imperfect manifestation of an ideal. With artefactual productions, we must see what is there, rather than reading through it to gain access to an imagined locus of intention.

Ælfric and the reproduction of homilies

The tension I have identified between a paradigm of production and an ideology of reproduction appears to have remained in force right through the Anglo-Saxon period, affecting even Ælfric, Anglo-Saxon England's most prolific author. Composed around the turn of the eleventh century, Ælfric's various authorial prefaces stand as a remarkable testament to one Anglo-Saxon perspective on the hazards of textual reproduction: Ælfric expresses the failures of the logic of the copy more clearly than any other Anglo-Saxon author. As a result, Ælfric often begs those who copy his books to copy correctly and correct new copies from the exemplars, and the Preface to the First Series of his *Catholic Homilies* sets the pattern for many of those which follow: 'Nu bydde ic and halsige on Godes naman, gif hwa þas boc awritan wylle, þæt he hi geornlice gerihte be ðære bysene, þy læs ðe we ðurh gymelease writeras geleahtrode beon. Mycel yfel deð se ðe leas writ, buton he hit gerihte, swylce he gebringe þa soðan lare to leasum gedwylde' ('Now I bid and pray in God's name, if anyone wishes to write this book [again], that he eagerly correct it by the exemplar, lest we be brought to blame by careless writers. He who writes falsely does great harm, unless he correct it, as he brings true teaching to false heresy').[40] Frequently, as here, Ælfric associates textual error with spiritual error, in an effort to manage the future correctness (and hence spiritual value) of his texts according to his own perceptions. More than any other Anglo-Saxon example I am aware of, however, Ælfric's comments indicate that he sees the copy as inferior to the original, and his requests for accuracy and correction should be seen as a reflection of that understanding. Yet the insistence with which he asks his future copyists for accuracy and correction should probably also be taken as reflecting his understanding that such attention to precision ran against the grain of scribal habits in a culture that was dominated by the logic of production, rather than reproduction. One important way of reading Ælfric's prefaces, then, is as an attempt to impose and enforce the logic of textual reproduction in relation to his works, even in the face of his culture's predominant textual logic of production. Certainly, modern scholars have often noted just how ineffective Ælfric's prefaces were in enforcing such a textual media perspective.

It is notable, however, that in both his Latin and Old English prefaces, Ælfric deploys the traditions for defining his texts as texts via paratextual apparatus as we have seen them used by Bede and Alfred: his prefaces usually take the form of letters, they generally attach his name (and often his position of authority 'alumnus Aðelwoldi', 'munuc and mæssepreost', 'abbas Egneshamnensibus', 'abbod'), and they sometimes

---

[40] Jonathan Wilcox, ed., *Ælfric's Prefaces* (Durham: Durham Medieval Texts, 1994), p. 110.

include titles for the works in question (*Genesis, Grammatica*).[41] In some cases, his prefatory remarks take great care to delineate the extent of Ælfric's texts: in the Preface to Genesis, Ælfric specifies just how much of the book he translates (from the beginning up to Isaac); in the Preface to the Second Series of the *Catholic Homilies*, he notes that each of those two collections contains exactly forty items. Once again, we see the deployment of author's name, title, and issues of textual definition in the service of textual reproduction.

But Ælfric's interests in or anxieties about textual reproduction go at least one step further at the end of the Old English Preface to *The Lives of Saints*, where he writes,

> Ic bidde nu   on Godes naman,
> gif hwa þas boc   awritan wille
> þæt he hi wel gerihte   be þære bysne,
> and þær na mare   betwux ne sette
> þonne we awendon.   Vale in Domino.

('I pray now in God's name, if someone wishes to write this book, that he correct it well by the exemplar, and set no more within it there than we translated. Farewell in the Lord').[42] Here, Ælfric's concern with textual boundaries comes to the foreground, and he explicitly discourages the inclusion of unauthorized non-Ælfrician items within the collection, although even the best manuscript of the collection that survives seems to include four items that modern scholars have identified as intrusive. It may well be significant that *The Lives of Saints* is Ælfric's most extensive collection of late Old English verse, and that at least one of the intrusive items, *The Legend of the Seven Sleepers*, appears to be at least partially in late Old English verse itself: Ælfric may well have recognized that Old English verse, as a genre, was especially likely to attract additional texts and accretions.[43] We must recall that all four of the classical Old English 'poetic codices' were likely to have been compiled in the generation

---

[41] Wilcox, *Ælfric's Prefaces*, pp. 107, 108, 123, 124, 116, 115.

[42] Wilcox, *Ælfric's Prefaces*, p. 121, relineated to show verse structure: if we take alliteration on prepositions as functional in Ælfric, as seems to be justified, only the fourth of these lines lacks alliteration, and it does show an alliterative link with the previous line. For Ælfric as poet (and for the metrical rules he follows) see Thomas A. Bredehoft, *Early English Metre* (Toronto: University of Toronto Press, 2005), pp. 81–90.

[43] On the presence of verse in *The Seven Sleepers*, see Thomas A. Bredehoft, *Authors, Audiences, and Old English Verse* (Toronto: University of Toronto Press, 2009), pp. 185–8.

before and during Ælfric's flourishing, and the poems within them
exhibit boundary problems of various kinds, as described above.

But it bears reiterating that Ælfric's failure to control the future state
of his texts exemplifies the power of the cultural logic of book production that was operative during the Anglo-Saxon period. The popularity
of Ælfric's homilies led to their very widespread dissemination indeed,
but individual homilies and saints' lives were frequently recombined
into other collections and individual homilies were sometimes modified
into composite homilies. Further, the controlling prefaces were often
simply dropped from later manuscripts of his works. Of course, the act
of dropping the prefaces served to sever the controlling paratextual
apparatus from the Ælfrician texts, presenting them as essentially anonymous compositions, ripe for remaking into new productions, suited for
new audiences. While Ælfric certainly understands the power of paratextual material (including the author's name) as contributing to textual
stability and identity, his early readers often reframed (or deframed) his
works into the anonymous mode. Detaching the paratextual apparatus,
including the authorial name, in these cases, served to free Ælfric's sermons in particular from the historical positioning that helped to define
them as texts: these sermons and homilies, whose very usefulness to
later readers lay in their ability to be reused in later times and other
places, were more useful as anonymous works than as authored ones,
just as the lack of textual identity offered by anonymous works made
them more ripe for recontextualization, recombination, and rewriting.
Significantly, the prefaces to Genesis and *The Grammar* survive much
more frequently than the prefaces to the *Catholic Homilies*, both of which
survive in only a single manuscript.[44]

The de-authoring of Ælfric's homilies and their reuse in composite
collections and individual items are two sides of a single coin: stripping
the paratextual material from Ælfric's works had the fortunate effect of
clouding or obscuring their nature as texts, making them instead into
productions or artefacts whose usefulness lay in recycling, recombination,

---

[44] As indicated by Wilcox, *Ælfric's Prefaces*, at p. 74: 'The prefaces to both the First and
Second Series of *Catholic Homilies* survive only in MS CUL, Gg. 3. 28'; at p. 77: 'Of the ten
more or less full medieval manuscripts of the *Grammar*, the prefaces survive in six'; and
at p. 78: 'Ælfric's translation of the first half of Genesis survives more or less complete in
two different versions, in a total of three manuscripts, all of which originally circulated
with the preface.'

and reuse in other productions. It is probably appropriate to see the recycling of Ælfric's homilies as analogous to the reuse of older manuscripts as binding materials: an act of making, of production, in which older artefacts were reused to make something new. Such an analogy strikingly encourages us to recognize that Ælfric attempts to inscribe his texts within a textual medium, but later book-makers see their manuscripts as examples of an artefactual kind of book. Tempting as it is to think of media as technologies, the Anglo-Saxon period, and the especially clear case of Ælfric's homilies, reminds us that media are a combination of specific technologies and the current ideas or ideologies that surround them. During the Anglo-Saxon period, the ink-on-vellum technology of the manuscript book supported two quite different modes, one textual and medial, and one artefactual: the artefactual mode appears to have been the more dominant.

Conclusions

What is most remarkable about the Anglo-Saxon examples discussed in this chapter is the regularity with which they functioned in their original context as dominated by the ideology of singular literary and visual production, rather than reproduction. Whether we consider the singularity of the *Beowulf* manuscript, the lack of authorial attribution for most Old English works, the relationship between *Daniel* and *Azarias*, the long history of additions to *The Anglo-Saxon Chronicle*, or the active de-authoring of Ælfric's homilies, an understanding of how the logic of production operates in each case offers us real insight into both the nature and the history of the works themselves. At the same time, the use and reuse of items from a particular suite of paratextual strategies (preface in the form of a letter; title; author's name; explicit statements of textual boundaries) exemplifies the very real traditionality of an alternative ideology of textual reproduction that was also current, if less dominant. Our understanding of works from the Anglo-Saxon period must begin, I think, with a consideration of how each work fits into the dynamic structured by the conflicting attitudes of these two traditional ways of conceptualizing book-making and textual making of all kinds.

The results of such a consideration, I hope to emphasize, may well be disorienting, so familiar is the assumption made by people in our culture

that media (including medieval manuscripts) are inherently reproductive in their ideological orientation: we habitually talk and write of manuscript 'copies' and 'copyists', after all. But it is important to recall that the
person responsible for the *Beowulf* manuscript almost certainly did not
see himself or herself as engaged in the work of copying. By way of a single concrete example (though many might have been chosen), we might
consider *Beowulf* line 1073, which appears in the manuscript as

    beloren leofum   æt þam hildplegan

('lost to loved ones at the battle-play'). Almost all editions of the poem,
of course, print 'lindplegan' (shield-play) as the final word of the line,
assuming that alliteration must link the two half-lines of the line together,
and assuming scribal error at some stage in the transmission. But such a
position, of course, sees scribal change as harmful to the text, articulating the author as the locus of textual authority. This is the operation of a
way of reading that takes the mode of textual reproduction as paradigmatic. It is perfectly possible to read line 1073 as a line produced by the
scribe for an early eleventh-century moment: the morpheme 'hild' may
be less archaic, and more lexically transparent, than 'lind' and thus easier
for an eleventh-century audience to parse. Likewise, standards of alliteration in the early eleventh century clearly allowed double alliteration
in the a-line (AA-alliteration) as a sufficient alliterative link, as seen in
the *Chronicle* poems as early as 975.[45] In short, it is perfectly plausible to
believe that the scribe responsible for the manuscript at this point may
have felt that line 1073 was acceptably formed as it stands, just as the
Beowulf scribes seem to have been willing to update the script and spelling of the poem to (or at least towards) contemporary standards. Our
entire theoretical perspective on which aspects of a medieval text are
'substantive' and which are 'accidentals' is built upon an understanding
of scribal activity as inherently reproductive, in the sense that it sepa-
rates authors from scribes as separate (and hierarchical) loci of authority. This is not to say that the *Beowulf* scribes never made errors—all
hand-work runs the risk of an occasional slip-up—but that modern
readers of the *Beowulf* manuscript should appropriately consider the
possibility that what our perspective identifies as non-authorial has historically been derived from an anachronistic position which sees scribal

---

[45] Bredehoft, *Early English Metre*, pp. 78–9.

activity as reproductive. Anglo-Saxons, very probably including the *Beowulf* scribes, habitually thought in terms of production, rather than reproduction, and our editorial and interpretive practices must rethink the implications of their practice.

More troubling, perhaps, are the difficulties in relating Anglo-Saxon texts to Anglo-Saxon culture. To understand the Ruthwell or Brussels Cross poems as 'quotations' from *The Dream of the Rood* asserts the cultural dissemination of something a great deal like the Vercelli poem: a quotation demands recognition by the audience, which takes the form of a deferral of authority onto the quoted (original) text. The only evidence for the cultural dissemination of the poem beyond the Vercelli book, of course, is precisely the evidence in question: the Brussels and Ruthwell crosses. If the audiences for these crosses do not know the Vercelli version, the crosses take on their own, strictly local and undeferred, authority. The relationship among the poems is undeniable, but to understand two of them as quotations involves a perspective on authority that denies that each work is a unique, independent production. To take any uniquely surviving Old English poem, and to understand it as exemplifying or embodying anything other than a strictly local cultural relevance, may be to invoke a vision of widespread familiarity that can only be justified by imagining a reproductive mode of textual multiplication and dissemination. But the evidence seems to suggest that books that were produced and reproduced in that mode were the exception rather than the rule, and that they ran against the grain of the norms of Anglo-Saxon textual practice.

Most disorienting of all, perhaps, are the implications of the use of paratextual apparatus by Bede, Alfred, and Ælfric in an attempt (not always successful) to bring their texts into the realm of reproduction. As all of these authors' works demonstrate, the logic of reproduction in this period was understood as dependent upon (or at least intertwined with) a definition of text as authored; historically localized, but aimed at a non-local audience; and bounded. The regularity with which these functions are articulated through a fairly consistent paratextual apparatus is remarkable in its own right, as well as remarkable for how closely it approximates the ways in which our own culture articulates authorship, audience, and textual boundaries in relation to literary works. Part of the attraction that Bede, Alfred, and Ælfric have for modern readers is precisely their seeming modernity.

But as I have argued here, those manuscript items that lack all or most of these paratextual materials have, as a result, such fluidly articulated textual boundaries and identities that they can only approximately be labelled as 'texts' at all. To put it another way, the articulation of textual boundaries in the Anglo-Saxon period is so clearly tied up in the notions of textual reproduction that it forces us to recognize anew how powerfully our own sense of textual definition is dependent upon an understanding of textual reproduction as the dominant paradigm. Old English productions—notably including nearly all classical Old English verse, but also *The Anglo-Saxon Chronicle* manuscripts, and the de-authored homilies of Ælfric—are not really texts, according to what we understand the word 'text' to mean, precisely because texts, for us, are subject to the logic of the copy. The insistence with which we attach titles, attempt authorial attributions, and define patterns of borrowing or composite structure to these items exemplifies our desire to make these productions into texts as we know them. It hardly seems necessary to note that we do these things most often precisely when we reproduce these items for our own consumption. But at some crucial level, we literally make these manuscript items into texts through our own definitional strategies: in their manuscript contexts, where those definitional strategies are so clearly avoided, the same items do not really function as 'texts' at all. To read literature from the Anglo-Saxon period, we must develop a reading strategy that can do without the idea of 'text' and that replaces it with the notion of productions in the artefactual mode. What the Anglo-Saxon period reveals most clearly is that our very understanding of the nature of a 'text' is predicated upon a vision of textuality as reproductive. And while Derrida appears to imagine that all of Western culture sees writing as medial, the Anglo-Saxon ability to see written works as productions suggests a resistance to, or freedom from, the logic of the copy that dominates the medial understanding of textuality.

I believe, in the end, that the recognition that the Anglo-Saxon period was primarily populated by textual productions and artefacts, rather than 'texts', urges us to adopt a dual perspective as modern readers. On the one hand, reading *Beowulf* as a text remains a productive strategy: the surviving manuscript still has much of value to tell us about the nature of its presumptive exemplar or exemplars. But our readings of Anglo-Saxon textual items need also to be accompanied by acts of seeing: the scripts of the *Beowulf* manuscript were very probably intended to give it a more-or-less up-to-date look and feel, and if we fail to attend to its up-to-dateness in order to focus on a reconstructed authorial version, we treat it *only* as a text, because such a reading practice devalues the production in front of us in favour of the 'work' which the manuscript supposedly can reflect only imperfectly. In Fred C. Robinson's famous phrase, the manuscript is the 'most immediate context' for much Anglo-Saxon literature; but even such a perspective reinscribes the hierarchy between text and context (or paratext) that is part and parcel of the reproductive 'logic of the copy'.[46] We must quite literally look at (and see, and even feel) manuscripts not as contextual travellers that accompany and support texts, but rather as productions and artefacts in their own right. We must both read them and see them.

[46] Fred C. Robinson, 'Old English Literature in its Most Immediate Context', in John D. Niles, ed., *Old English Literature in Context* (Cambridge: D. S. Brewer, 1980), pp. 11–29.

Interlude 1

Anglo-Saxon to Gothic

On 29 December 1170, Archbishop Thomas Becket was murdered in Canterbury Cathedral, shocking the twelfth-century Christian world and leading to his rapid canonization (1173) as a martyred English saint. The shock of the Christian world was at least partially enabled by the twelfth century's flourishing textual culture, which allowed both books and news to travel across the continent with a speed that must have been almost unthinkable even a century earlier. In the early eleventh century, after all, another Archbishop of Canterbury had been even more spectacularly martyred (in 1011) by marauding Danes, and although Alfheah was also duly canonized, it took until 1078, and his cult never approached the pan-European phenomenon that Becket's death prompted.[1] Something had changed in the intervening century and a half: Europe (and perhaps England in particular) had become largely Gothicized, and the rapid dissemination of both news and outrage about the Becket incident was enabled by a paradigm of visual and textual reproduction that had firmly established its roots in the preceding decades.

---

[1] The death of Becket is widely known, but Alfheah (sometimes spelled 'Elphege') is probably less familiar. The outlines of his story can be found in Nicholas Brooks, *The Early History of the Church of Canterbury* (London: Leicester University Press, 1996), pp. 278–85.

In modern literary circles, at least, 'Gothic' is a term that is all too rarely used, except perhaps in relation to vampires and certain kinds of romance narratives, but the term 'Gothic' very usefully captures one powerful component of much of the aesthetic expression of the later middle ages. As I understand it, the Gothic aesthetic embodies an appreciation for the repetition of certain distinct visual elements, usually squarishly vertical, bounded, and pointy. But the nature of Gothic repetition also involves intentional variation within the repetition, with each iteration including slight but meaningful differences that prevent the repetition from seeming overly mechanical and that also allow local, individual meanings. Whether we think of Gothic architecture, with its arches, columns, stained-glass windows, and flying buttresses, or of Gothic letter formation, with its prominent marking of the shoulder line and foot line in its sequences of minims, the emphasis on slight but significant variation within almost identical repetition is plain. A casual walk through the choir of almost any Gothic cathedral will bring the visual power of the repeated structures prominently to one's notice, but a closer look will usually reveal that each choir stall's misericord has a carving unique and different from every other one, just as the stained-glass windows may all have the same shape while showing images that are each unique. The Gothic aesthetic takes its power from the tension between the idea of identical repetition and the individual expressions that crop up irresistibly within or upon the seemingly identical elements.

After his death, Becket, no more unique and singular in his life or martyrdom than Alfheah, was reproduced almost endlessly: not only did the story of his death circulate widely, but so, too, did his image, in the form of pilgrim badges, ampullae, and other signs and tokens. The Gothicization of English and European culture in the twelfth century affected both visual and textual culture, and the Gothic aesthetic of visual repetition both expresses and demonstrates the new prominence of reproduction, rather than production, as the dominant ideological mode. At the risk of oversimplifying matters, it is nevertheless useful to see Alfheah as typical of his Anglo-Saxon time and place, a unique, one-off, individual person and production, most significant to his own local neighbourhood and audience. Becket, on the other hand, is a prototypically Gothic saint, subject to reproduction from the start, his presence literally spread out across the whole of Europe, and probably even

further: ampullae loaded with Becket's blood were dispersed as souvenirs to pilgrims from every corner of Christendom, its essence attenu-
ated by dilution in water, though no dilution could remove the nature of
that essence in the minds of believers in its efficacy. Each droplet of
Becket's blood remained, no doubt, unique and individual, and yet par-
took of the wholeness of Becket's sanctity: unique individuality within a
widely reproduced and distributed sameness.

| 2 |

Gothic Textual Reproduction

Before Geoffrey Chaucer's death in 1400, or shortly thereafter, his own scribe, Adam Pinkhurst, produced two manuscripts of *The Canterbury Tales*, known today as the Ellesmere manuscript and the Hengwrt manuscript.[1] Yet the two manuscripts, famously, have quite radically different orderings for the *Tales*, which has caused no end of critical and readerly uncertainty about what might have caused one scribe to have two such different ideas about the nature of the work.[2] One popular guess has been that both books were produced after Chaucer's death, meaning that the poet had left no authorial draft, and the scribe was simply trying to make the best of what Chaucer had left unfinished and disordered. Mooney's identification of the scribe as Pinkhurst, which strengthens the possibility that one or both books might have been made before Chaucer's death, however, suggests that Chaucer's death might not be to blame.

---

[1] See Linne R. Mooney, 'Chaucer's Scribe', *Speculum* 86 (2006), 97–138. The Hengwrt manuscript is Aberystwyth, National Library of Wales, Peniarth 392 D, and the Ellesmere manuscript is San Marino, CA, Huntington Library, Ellesmere 26 C 9. For the possibility that both books were made during Chaucer's lifetime, see the studies referenced in Mooney, 'Chaucer's Scribe', fn. 2, p. 97.

[2] As summarized in Larry D. Benson, ed., *The Riverside Chaucer*, 3rd edition (Boston: Houghton Mifflin, 1987), p. 1121, the Ellesmere book includes the ten 'fragments' of *The Tales* in order I–X, while Hengwrt's order is I, III, II, *Squire's Tale, Merchant's Tale, Franklin's Tale, Second Nun's Tale, Clerk's Tale*, VI, VII, IX, X.

How, though, could Chaucer (or even Adam Pinkhurst) have allowed two such different orderings for the tales? The answer seems both obvious and somewhat troubling in its implications, at least from our modern perspective: the author, Geoffrey Chaucer, may well not have had a consistent intention for *The Canterbury Tales* that could serve an authorizing or controlling function for the text of the *Tales*. We might, indeed, be tempted to speculate that each manuscript of the *Tales* (or at least each of these two manuscripts) was an individual production, manufactured entirely outside the ideology of reproduction, like the *Beowulf* manuscript, as I argued in the preceding chapter. But, of course, *The Canterbury Tales* has an author (Chaucer), whose name is prominent in the paratextual apparatus (the headings, incipits, and explicits of *Sir Thopas* and *Melibee* insistently name the pilgrim-narrator as Chaucer), and indeed, the whole of *The Tales* plays with paratextual prologues, narrators, and narratorial control in so many ways that it clearly lies fully within the paratextual definition of text. Likewise, Chaucer's separate poem addressed directly to 'Adam Scriveyn' is founded upon the logic of the copy, as Adam is admonished to 'wryte more trewe' in his future scribal activities.[3] Chaucer's immersion in medial textuality is unavoidable: the differences between Hengwrt and Ellesmere cannot derive from their status as individual and separate productions, but somehow both books function within the Gothic mode of medial, textual reproduction.

It will be my argument in this chapter that the proper understanding of the differences between Ellesmere and Hengwrt lies in recognizing more precisely just what it was that Gothic reproduction sought to reproduce. Modern textual theory (whether in the practice of textual critics, or in the ideology identified and interrogated by Derrida) generally understands that texts are medial because they stand between us and a perfect, but generally inaccessible, authoritative form. Gothic reproduction, I believe, also sees texts as medial, standing between readers and something that lies neither in books nor in authors nor in readers: but what Gothic reproductions usually attempt to reproduce is a moving target, a multiform, rather than a singular perfect form. The blood of Becket could be endlessly

---

[3] The poem, *Chaucer's Wordes unto Adam, his Owne Scriveyn*, is found in Benson, ed., *The Riverside Chaucer*, p. 650; the quotation is from line 4. Throughout, I cite poems by Chaucer from this edition.

reproduced via dilution, Becket's sanctity standing as the literally transcendent signifier that could authorize and guarantee the value, purity, and meaning of the reproduction. But in the more worldly world of books, literature, and visual culture—and even in the very ampullae that contained and transmitted Becket's blood—the ideology of Gothic reproduction operated largely without a reliance on any equivalently transcendent original text. In its place stood a Gothic innovation: the 'moving target' original.

As an ideology, Gothic reproduction powerfully depends upon the logic of the copy, in which copies always fail as representations, and part of that failure could indeed derive from what might legitimately be called error, as Chaucer's *Wordes unto Adam* indicates. Even so, it is crucial to recognize that not all scribal interventions can be categorized as error: some spelling changes, for example, are likely to be value-neutral altera-tions. Further scribal variations based in dialect—whether the scribe's, commissioner's, or patron's—may well have been both typical and expected. In the absence of obvious, manifest error, many of the sorts of textual variation that we can discover through collation were probably both undetectable and acceptable: moving target originals, in this sense, generate what Bernard Cerquiglini has labelled textual *variance* almost as a matter of course. While Cerquiglini's dictum, 'medieval writing does not produce variants; it *is* variance' may seem somewhat cryptic,[4] I believe it captures quite precisely the Gothic ideology of the moving tar-get original. Each medieval scribe, in the absence of an ideological con-ception of an original that has a unique, authorizing form, felt free to produce copies that varied from their exemplars at virtually every level. It may be the case, as Cerquiglini has suggested, that such *variance* is especially characteristic of vernacular texts,[5] but outside of sacred and legal domains, where the authorizing, controlling effects of originals expressed themselves most powerfully, even Latin works, I believe, were understood to have moving target originals, perhaps especially in the realm of literature.

We must recognize, then, the degree to which the supposed failure of Gothic copies derives from the 'moving target' nature of authorial intent,

[4] Bernard Cerquiglini, *In Praise of the Variant: A Critical History of Philology*, trans. Betsy Wing (Baltimore: Johns Hopkins University Press, 1999), pp. 77–8.
[5] Cerquiglini, *In Praise of the Variant*, pp. 37–8.

whether as a real force in the world (Chaucer's actual intentions) or as a structuring principle of texts (what a text is intended or understood to be). Two copies of a 'moving target' original could differ from one another in larger or smaller ways (orthography, diction, *ordinatio*, completeness, contents), without either copy being understood as a greater or lesser failure. Ellesmere and Hengwrt differ from one another at all of these levels, and we might indeed ask whether Ellesmere represents Chaucer's final intention more accurately than Hengwrt, but it is also perfectly plausible to suppose that both might closely represent stages in Chaucer's intention.[6] Our desire or expectation that one moment of Chaucer's evolving intention has precedence or priority over all others can hardly coexist with a real world in which the making of a book like Hengwrt or Ellesmere must have literally taken weeks or months, unless we understand Chaucer as making use of a self-imposed deadline, after which he would never again alter the text or intent of his work. Of course, Chaucer's death would indeed provide a suitable deadline, for our purposes of textual definition, if not for Chaucer's, but as we shall see, the remarkable continuations of Lydgate and the Beryn-poet, to say nothing of various other later compilers of *The Tales*, exemplify how, within Gothic reproduction, even the death of the author could not really fix the intent of the text, at least according to our terms. A clearer understanding of the ideology of textual and visual reproduction in the Gothic middle ages will prove valuable indeed for our understanding of even the most familiar authors and texts.

This chapter, then, will begin by sketching out the evidence that suggests that the ideology of reproduction did come to predominate over the ideology of production in the twelfth century, thereafter maintaining its dominance (though never entirely removing the ideology of production from circulation) throughout the later middle ages. But unlike the truly mechanical reproduction of the later print era, Gothic reproduction accepted, and even traded upon, the vital necessity of individual, local variation that made each iteration unique. As we shall see, whether considering *variance* in late medieval texts, the practice (and the literary

---

[6] For a recent defence of Ellesmere as an authoritative book that 'brings us, in some ways, as close as we can get to the figure of its creator' see A. S. G. Edwards, 'The Ellesmere Manuscript: Controversy, Culture, and the *Canterbury Tales*', in Orietta Da Rold and Elaine Treharne, eds., *Textual Cultures: Cultural Texts* (Cambridge: D. S. Brewer, 2010), pp. 59–73 (quotation from p. 73).

topos) of translation, or the textual diversity of surviving manuscripts of Chaucer and Langland, or even the interwoven visual domains of manuscripts, stained glass, and pilgrim badges, the Gothic aesthetic of variation within iteration dominated the period in important ways.

Twelfth-century developments

In his admirable survey of Canterbury ampullae and badges, Brian Spencer recounts how the monks of Canterbury seem to have almost immediately hit on the notion of distributing and selling Becket's blood, thoroughly diluted in water. 'Within two or three years of his martyrdom', Spencer notes, 'ampullae were already universally recognized as souvenirs from Canterbury.'[7] Often large and elaborate, even ostentatious, Canterbury ampullae were moulded from tin in stone moulds, and words and text were often included.[8] The earliest Canterbury ampullae usually show some variation on a Latin text such as 'Optimus egrorum medicus fit Toma bonorum' ('Thomas makes the best doctor of the goodly sick').[9] As early as the early thirteenth century, however, artistic control of the badges seems to have slipped, perhaps due to high demand for badges; alternatively, we might rather say that textual variation or *variance* begins to exert itself by the early thirteenth century. Spencer's example 12, from the Vintry site in London (the location helps establish the date), shows an inscription which is 'entirely garbled'.[10] Although Spencer does not attempt a transcription, his photograph shows an inscription that surely must be read as pseudo-textual: it is not clear that all the characters are actual letters, and others appear to be either retrograde, inverted, or both.

Importantly, even as a pseudo-text, it is likely that the visible text on Spencer's Vintry ampulla functioned in context as a medial text. In the terms used by G. Thomas Tanselle, a prominent theorist of textual criticism, a text is a set of 'instructions' for producing a work in the medium of language, and even the garbled Vintry text appears to operate in

---

[7] Brian Spencer, *Pilgrim Souvenirs and Secular Badges: Medieval Finds from Excavations in London* (London: The Stationery Office, 1998), p. 39.

[8] Spencer, *Pilgrim Souvenirs*, p. 39.

[9] See Spencer, *Pilgrim Souvenirs*, examples 5, 6, and 9, on pp. 47–53.

[10] Spencer, *Pilgrim Souvenirs*, p. 53.

context as a text according to Tanselle's definition.[11] That is to say, even if the visible signs of the Vintry text cannot be construed as letters, it seems likely that the pseudo-textual inscription was understood by the owner (and probably the seller) as referencing 'Optimus egrorum medicus fit Toma bonum' or some other phrase. Our inability to follow these particular instructions with confidence does not mean that they did not function effectively in context; indeed, it seems likely that they did, though not through the means of literal construal.[12] The logic of the copy is manifest here: whether we see the Vintry ampulla as a faulty copy of an earlier badge or simply note that its physical text is a faulty physical manifestation of a linguistic work, we are firmly in the realm of visual and textual reproduction and its concomitant failures.

But perhaps we can tease the implications of such an example out a bit further. When confronted with a pseudo-text such as that found on this Vintry ampulla, sellers and buyers of such items presumably understood what they saw as a text and shared its content with one another. By an act of collation and comparison with other surviving ampullae, we can hypothesize the linguistic 'work' lying behind the Vintry pseudo-text as something like 'Optimus egrorum medicus fit Toma bonum'. But the twelfth- or thirteenth-century individuals involved might well have agreed on some other meaning, likely even something in English, rather than Latin. This problem of potential translation or multilingual expression is no doubt operative with well-formed Latin badge inscriptions as well, as the seemingly popular market and audience for such objects and texts may indicate that the sharing of the meaning or sense of these scripts often took place in the various European vernaculars. Although we can hypothesize that the dynamic of textual reproduction involved in such cases identifies the 'text' manifested on a particular object as a (faulty) copy of a linguistic form or 'work', such a hypothesis is not especially useful for understanding either the badge-texts themselves or their

---

[11] G. Thomas Tanselle, *A Rationale of Textual Criticism* (Philadelphia: University of Pensylvania Press, 1989), pp. 11–38. Tanselle's eloquent explication of the principles of textual criticism identifies a 'text' according to its participation in a particular act of reproduction: a text is a physical record of or set of instructions intended to generate a performance of a (literary) work in the medium of language, much like a musical score is a set of instructions for the creation of a work of music.

[12] Thomas A. Bredehoft, 'Literacy without Letters: Pilgrim Badges and Late-Medieval Literate Ideology', *Viator* 37 (2006), 433–45.

function in context, because a single (pseudo-) text might have been voiced in a variety of ways: if Tanselle's claim that a text is a set of directions for producing a work is applicable here, pseudo-textual badges (and therefore others as well) might have served to generate the voicing of a variety of such works. The limits of Tanselle's position, I think, become visible in such examples: some texts, necessarily including these Gothic texts, were produced in an environment of textual reproduction, and they were clearly subject to the logic of the copy (which can account for their very faultiness), but the 'works' which lie behind these texts do not have the power or coherence of Platonic ideals. The seller or owner of the Vintry ampulla who declares that it reads 'Optimus egrorum medicus fit Toma bonorum' is no more correct or incorrect than the individual who says it reads 'Thomas makeþ þe best fisicien' or even 'Thomas est un bon physicien.' The pseudo-textual script, because of its very linguistic indeterminacy, is especially subject to translation, reproducible in multiple languages. Even imagining a single authorizing form as lying behind the Vintry pseudo-text appears to ignore the reality of the context, which allows the textual instructions to produce multiple messages in multiple languages.

Such badges would be mere curiosities, I think, if it were not for the way in which they function as reproductive scripts for which there is *and can be* no stable or coherent controlling 'original'. The pseudo-textual script, indeed, makes use of the logic of the copy to visually imply an underlying original which can be given voice, but it resists or refuses any specification of that original. Unlike the simulacrum, the copy for which there is no original at all, Gothic pseudo-texts like the Vintry ampulla make use of the necessity of an original, but they operate by defining that original as variable and multiform, as a moving target.[13] The 'moving target original' is the defining characteristic of Gothic textuality; ideally, such originals generate copies that are largely identical in each iteration, but with necessary, even beautiful or remarkable, local individuality. Although tracing the evolution of such an

---

[13] See Jean Baudrillard, *Simulations*, trans. Paul Foss, Paul Patton, and Philip Beitchman (New York: Semiotext(e), 1983). Simulacra also challenge or play with the logic of the copy, but the 'moving target' texts I have in mind in this chapter seem structurally different. A simulacrum operates with nothing at all in the 'original' position, suggesting the autonomy of the medium itself, while Gothic reproductions depend upon something being in the 'original' position, playing upon its inaccessibility or instability, rather than its absence.

ideology may prove impossible, it seems likely that the multilingual aspect of the pseudo-textual problem may relate to the prominence of translation as a characteristic concern of Gothic literature from its very beginnings.

Earlier in the twelfth century, half a century before the death of Becket, and perhaps following the lead of Bede, twelfth-century Anglo-Norman writers such as William of Malmesbury, John of Worcester, and Henry of Huntingdon all began writing Latin histories for Anglo-Norman audiences, beginning probably in the 1120s.[14] All three, notably, engaged in translation; all three used the Old English *Anglo-Saxon Chronicle* as an important source for their histories. Writing for multiple, distant audiences, all three (like Bede) understood their works to be taking place within the ideological realm of reproduction (rather than production), and it hardly seems necessary to point out that all three are named authors, with named works that are accompanied by a complex paratextual apparatus. But importantly, the translational mode seems to echo or reinforce the investment of these authors' works in the ideology of reproductive textuality: as an activity, translation paradigmatically invokes the logic of the copy, as the (translated) copy manifestly must fail to completely match the original. A translation is, more or less by definition, a medial representation, at least in so far as it openly acknowledges its status as a translation.

Around 1138, when he seems to have published his *History of the Kings of Britain*, Geoffrey of Monmouth seems to have explicitly recognized how this newly prominent mode of writing for a widespread audience depended upon a kind of simultaneous translation and reproduction. Citing at the very beginning of his history 'a certain very ancient book in the British language' supposedly loaned to him by Walter, Archdeacon of Oxford, Geoffrey identifies his own great work as a translation of a vernacular work pretty much completely inaccessible to his own readers.[15] Geoffrey returns to a discussion of his source-book at the very end of his

---

[14] Many of the arguments presented here and in the next few paragraphs were first presented, in very different form, in Thomas A. Bredehoft, 'The Gothic Turn in Twelfth-Century English Chronicles', in Elaine Treharne and Greg Walker, eds., *The Oxford Handbook of Medieval Literature in English* (Oxford: Oxford University Press, 2010), pp. 353–69.

[15] Michael A. Faletra, ed. and trans., *Geoffrey of Monmouth: The History of the Kings of Britain* (Broadview: Peterborough, ON, 2008), p. 41.

own book, where the logic of the copy is explicit: William of Malmesbury and Henry of Huntingdon, Geoffrey suggests, should steer clear of
British history since they do not have access to Geoffrey's book, and the
translation of it that Geoffrey has made is apparently insufficient as a
substitute for the more authentic British original.[16] But to the degree that
Geoffrey cites an authenticating source which cannot be accessed or col-
lated by any of his readers, its very value as an authorizing or controlling
source is referenced here only ironically.

At this early Gothic moment in the 1130s, then, Geoffrey of Monmouth appears to recognize the inability of the ideal Gothic original to
offer a controlling original, because the very process of translation—
especially translation from a linguistically inaccessible original—is a
kind of reproduction that inevitably produces variety, rather than uniformity. Given his references to William of Malmesbury and Henry of
Huntingdon, both of whom cite *The Anglo-Saxon Chronicle* as an authorizing source, Geoffrey need not even remind his own readers explicitly
of the fact that their translations differ from one another: Gothic reproduction, imaginatively linked to translation from an early stage, must
recognize that originals cannot control copies perfectly, and that copies/
translations necessarily vary from one another, even while ostensibly
standing as versions/copies of the very same original. Notably, however,
while Geoffrey, William, and Henry all privilege a vernacular original as
authorizing and supporting their translations, it is important to remember that Wace translated Geoffrey's book into French before the end of
the twelfth century and Layamon translated Wace into English not much
later: Gothic issues of named authorship, translation, and reproduction
do not depend on a particular or unidirectional vernacular–Latin
dynamic. But the rampant success of Geoffrey of Monmouth's *History of
the Kings of Britain* apparently attests to the spirit of the twelfth-century's
engagement with Gothic reproduction, even as its own rapid dissemination may possibly have played a role in the spreading of classic Gothic
script.[17]

---

[16] Faletra, *History of the Kings of Britain*, p. 217.

[17] See Albert Derolez, *The Palaeography of Gothic Manuscript Books from the Twelfth to
the Early Sixteenth Century* (Cambridge: Cambridge University Press, 2003), p. 71, for the
suggestion that Gothic script may have spread from the Anglo-Norman kingdom during
the twelfth century.

As tempting as it might be to identify Geoffrey's literary exploitation of Gothic reproduction as an originary moment, the precise moment (or even decade) when the Anglo-Saxon culture of textual production was supplanted by the Gothic culture of reproduction probably cannot be established with any precision. Certainly, the recopying of ascriptionless Ælfrician homilies into and through the twelfth century argues for the continuity of the Anglo-Saxon perspective well after the origins of the Gothic perspective; the twelfth century was doubtless a time of transition, where the different modes operated simultaneously. Regardless, however, what translation, as a widespread literary practice, accomplishes most thoroughly is to insist upon the simultaneous existence of multiple 'copies' of the same book or text that are manifestly different from one another.

As a result, the linkage between translation and a view of textual activity as reproductive may also help clarify the twelfth-century blossoming of vernacular literatures: translation explicitly opens up a new audience for a text, and therefore the logic of translation is always about the expansion or multiplication of a work's audience. It is also clear that twelfth-century translation involved virtually all imaginable language contexts, even if we limit our consideration to the British Isles. Not only did William of Malmesbury, John of Worcester, and Henry of Huntingdon translate the *Anglo-Saxon Chronicle* (or parts of it) into Latin, but Gaimar also translated it into French. As noted above, Geoffrey of Monmouth's *Historia Regum Brittaniae* was translated into French (by Wace) shortly after the middle of the century, and thence into English (by Layamon) around the end of the century. Marie de France's writings claim to be translations into French from Breton (*Lais*), Old English (*Fables*), and Latin (*St Patrick's Purgatory*). Certainly some translation during this period was accomplished anonymously, but the prominence of these authors' and translators' names once more serves as a reminder of how these translations are generally (if not always) accompanied by a sophisticated paratextuality intended to establish authorship, textual identity and boundaries, and historical positioning. The case of Marie de France's *Lais* can be taken, not as typical, but as especially revealing.

Often seen as masterpieces of compositional efficiency, Marie's *Lais* examine the hot twelfth-century literary topic of love through a variety of engaging scenarios. Each *lai* is generally accompanied by a short preface and epilogue, clearly intended to demarcate the boundaries of each separate poem, and often containing more or less explicit commentary on the names of the various *lais*. The entire collection of twelve *lais* is headed by a substantial verse preface, and Marie's name is given (as 'Marie' only) in the separate preface to the first lay, *Guigemar*.[18] Compared with the largely anonymous presentation of Anglo-Saxon narrative poetry, the complexity and thoroughness of Marie's deployment of paratextual prefaces to define her texts' boundaries, identify their titles, and indicate her own name clearly marks a remarkable shift in vernacular poetics almost as important as the shift from English to French. But the verse prefaces (also naming the authors) which are attached to Layamon's *Brut* and Orm's *Ormulum* serve to suggest that English did not always lag behind French fashion in such matters by very much at all.

Along the way, however, Marie's comments in these paratextual prefaces articulate a fuller view of what is at stake in literary production and reproduction, as she sees it. In the preface to the collection as a whole, she writes:

> I began to think about making some good stories, and translating from Latin to French, but that would have brought me no reward: there are others engaged in that! I thought of the *lais* that I'd heard: I doubted not, and knew it well, that for the remembrance of adventures they had heard, those who first made them began them and sent them forth.[19]

Here, Marie chooses not to enter the fray of those who merely translate from Latin into French, as the rewards for such a common activity apparently lie below her aspirations. Instead, she chooses to translate from Breton, not because of the relative status of that language in relation to Latin, but presumably for its novelty or its inaccessibility. But Marie certainly discusses the origins and transmission of the *lais* here in

---

[18] *Guigemar*, l. 3; I cite Marie's *Lais* from Jean Rychner, ed., *Les Lais de Marie de France* (Paris: Éditions Champion, 1969). See, however, Cerquiglini, *In Praise of the Variant*, p. 29, who notes the references to 'Marie' here as well as in the *Fables* and *St Patrick's Purgatory*, to observe that 'From these three separate marks of an intradiegetic-heterodiegetic narrator (to use Gérard Genette's terms), an author has been created and endowed with the beautiful name Marie de France.'

[19] Marie de France, 'Prologue', ll. 28–38: 'Començai a penser/D'aukune bone estoire faire/E de latin en romaunz traire;/Mais ne me fust guaires de pris:/Itant s'en sunt altre entremis!/Des lais pensai, k'oïz aveie./Ne dutai pas, bien le saveie,/Ke pur remembrance les firent/Des aventures k'il oïrent/Cil ki primes les comencierent/E ki avant les enveierent.'

terms of reproduction: they were first made to preserve and transmit *aventures* that had previously been heard, and her own translations both serve those ends and extend the audience into the realm of French speakers and French readers. As this passage suggests, Marie understands the *lais* as partaking of the effects of a reproductive medium, whether the medium in question is the oral transmission of Breton *lais* or the literate and literary French couplets of her own translations.

Even more interestingly, Marie's *lais* often engage in deliberate play with their own paratexts: five of the twelve *lais* appear to be given at least two titles (*Bisclavret*, *Laüstic*, *Chaitivel*, *Chievrefoil*, and *Eliduc*), sometimes offering differing perspectives, and sometimes offering titles in different languages. The main characters in *Chaitivel* argue over the proper name of the *lai* even before it is composed, eventually agreeing that *Chaitivel* is the proper title, before Marie herself suggests, somewhat contrarily, 'each of the names suits it well'.[20] At the end of *Chievrefoil*, Marie implies that the original composition of the *lai* can be attributed to Tristram himself, one of the *lai*'s characters: 'Tristram, who well know how to play the harp, made a new lai about it; I'll name it quite briefly: the English call it *Goatleaf*; the French name it *Chievrefoil*.'[21] Neither the French nor the English title suits a supposed Breton original or even Tristram's presumably Cornish composition at all well. Translation here is identified explicitly as involving a kind of reproductive failure, and through its multiplication the defining function of the title is undermined for literary effect, just as the textual play serves to obscure or mock the authorizing effect of the translated original. Part of the Gothic effect of Marie's play with titles and translation involves poking fun at the unreliability of the inaccessible (Breton, oral) originals; her offering of multiple, contested titles exposes the failure of the paratextual function of the title to define the (translated) text. In the most obvious case—is *Chievrefoil* derived from a Celtic, French, or English original?—Marie clearly articulates her authorizing source as a moving target.

The textual history of the *lais*, it must be recalled, suggests the same conclusion: Rychner's manuscript H (Harley 978) is the only manuscript

---

[20] Marie de France, *Chaitivel*, l. 235: 'Chescuns des nuns bien i afiert.'

[21] Marie de Franve, *Chievrefoil*, ll. 112–16: 'Tristram, ki bien saveit harper,/En aveit fet un nuvel lai;/Asez briefment le numerai:/*Gotelef* l'apelent Engleis,' *Chievrefoil* le nument Franceis.

to include all twelve *lais* as well as the only one to include the overall prologue; two other manuscripts include multiple *lais,* and two further
manuscripts feature only one *lai* each. We may well presume that the
fullest manuscript best represents Marie's intention, but (as with the
Canterbury Tales manuscripts), it may be more accurate to note that in
the eyes of medieval book-makers, no single authorial intention seems
to have been determinative of the contents or even order of such a collection. And of course the manuscripts show a great deal of variation at
the local level as well. In the fourth line of *Lanval,* where the title of the
lai is given, the four manuscripts differ:

> H: en bretans l'apelent Lanval ('in Breton, they call it *Lanval*')
> P: en breton, l'apelent Lanval ('in Breton, they call it *Lanval*')
> C: en Bretaigne l'apelent Lanval ('in Brittany, they call it *Lanval*')
> S: Li Breton l'apelent Lanval ('the Bretons call it *Lanval*')[22]

H and P here differ only in spelling, but C and S involve more radical
changes, although all four readings certainly make acceptable sense.
Variations of these kinds, of course, are the norm in medieval manuscripts, where multiple copies exist, and while printed editions must
make a choice between readings, medieval scribes' choices do not clearly
seem to be driven by a need for adherence to an authorial, authoritative
original. The absence of the author-naming overall preface to the *Lais*
from three of these manuscripts might urge us to recall the de-authoring
of Ælfrician homilies discussed in the previous chapter, but Marie's play
with titles nevertheless suggests that the paradigm has indeed shifted:
the variation in manuscripts of *Lanval* (and the rest of the *Lais*) is not a
matter of their being a series of new productions, but rather a consequence of their existence as copies of a 'moving target' literary original.

Geoffrey of Monmouth's and Marie de France's literary investment in
a paradigm of textual reproduction is plain from their deployment of
authorial names and other definitive paratextual strategies, and both the
Historia Regum Brittaniae and *The Lais* certainly survive in multiple

---

[22] Manuscript H is London, British Library, Harley 978; S is Paris, Bibliothèque nationale, nouv. acq. fr. 1104; P is Paris, Bibliothèque nationale, fr. 2168; C is London, British
Library, Cotton Vespasian B. xiv. These manuscript readings are cited from the textual
notes in Rychner, ed., *Marie de France,* though I have left 'Lanval' in roman type, rather
than italicized, to remind my own readers that a translation like 'in Breton they call him
Lanval' remains possible for the line.

manuscripts. Both, however, by problematizing the inaccessible nature of their vernacular originals, identify their sources as failing to provide a stable, defining, authorizing target for the resulting Gothic reproductions. Driven, perhaps, by the recognition that translation always fails as a strategy of reproduction, Geoffrey and Marie recognize that that very failure opens the door for a kind of productive textual play or indeterminacy that I have characterized as demonstrating the 'moving target' nature of their implied sources. These twelfth-century authors, as I hope to show in succeeding sections, already exemplify the central dynamics of the Gothic mode: the variation-within-repetition Gothic aesthetic differs from the ideology of truly mechanical reproduction precisely in imagining a 'moving target' original that generates productive individual 'copies' that succeed on their own terms even as they differ from one another, as opposed to being ideologically condemned as failures.

Productions and Gothic reproductions

Even in the face of the predominant mode of Gothic reproduction, late medieval manuscript (and visual) culture continued to allow the singular production of unique literary and artistic artefacts. Indeed, Chaucer's great contemporary, the *Pearl*-poet, appears to have operated within a textual paradigm very little different from his Anglo-Saxon predecessors. No authorial name attaches to *Pearl*, *Sir Gawain and the Green Knight*, *Patience*, or *Purity*, and even those titles are purely modern. All four poems, then, survive without the kinds of paratextual apparatus that would serve to bound and define them, and it is surely no mere accident that all four poems survive to the present in only a single manuscript. As with the bulk of classical Old English poetry, the anonymity of these texts, their general lack of paratexts, and their unique survival all fit together to define their ideological status as singular literary artefacts or productions, written and presented to an apparently local audience without the active intention of placing them into wider circulation. The predominance of the Gothic mode of reproduction may have weakened the cultural prominence of such productions, but unique productions have always remained a possibility.

The example of the *Pearl*-poet, nevertheless, usefully contextualizes the reproductive nature of Chaucer and Langland's great poems. In the case of Langland's *Piers Plowman*, a poem which survives in more than fifty manuscripts with a truly bewildering variety of textual variation and *variance*, at every level, scholarship has traditionally identified no fewer than three major versions of the poem, labelled A, B, and C.[23] A fourth version, Z, possibly represents an 'original' version, and there are also various manuscripts that combine, for example, an A beginning with a C conclusion.[24] Indeed, the debates about the nature and number of 'versions' of the text have been extensive and vehement: whatever else we learn from the textual complexity of *Piers Plowman*, all readers must acknowledge that the hypothesis of a single authoritative version fits the reality of manuscript and textual diversity very poorly indeed.[25] In large part, the difficulty has been exacerbated by a continuing habit of distinguishing between textual variants that supposedly derive from scribes as opposed to those which might derive from the author. The identification of a series of moments in the history of *Piers Plowman* as authoritative (A, B, C, and so on), however, really serves most importantly to force a set of authorial deadlines upon the idea of the poem. However we label or define the stages in the poem's development, *Piers Plowman* forces us to confront the radical ways in which its participation in a paradigm of reproduction fails to rely upon a singular controlling or defining authoritative version.

[23] The A, B, and C versions were first given these labels in the important nineteenth-century editions of W. W. Skeat; see especially, W. W. Skeat, ed., *The Vision of William Concerning Piers the Plowman in Three Parallel Texts* (Oxford: Oxford University Press, 1886). The hypothesis of three versions has been reinforced in the controversial and important Athlone editions, as well as in the critical tradition at large: see George Kane, ed., *Piers Plowman: The A Version* (London: Athlone Press, 1960); George Kane and E. Talbot Donaldson, eds., *Piers Plowman: The B Version* (London: Athlone Press, 1975); and George Russell and George Kane, eds., *Piers Plowman: The C Version* (London: Athlone Press, 1997).

[24] The Z version has been published in facsimile, accompanied by introductory essays, in Charlotte Brewer and A. G. Rigg, *Piers Plowman: A Facsimile of the Z-Text in Bodleian Library Oxford, MS Bodley* 851 (Cambridge: D. S. Brewer, 1994). In Bodley 851, in fact, the Z-version is also accompanied by a C-type ending.

[25] Lawrence Warner, *The Lost History of* Piers Plowman (Philadelphia: University of Pennsylvania Press, 2011) is just one recent work to radically reconceive the conventional scholarly story of the versions of *Piers Plowman*; see also C. David Benson, *Public Piers Plowman: Modern Scholarship and Late Medieval English Culture* (Philadelphia: University of Pennsylvania Press, 2004), pp. 43–75 for his discussion of 'the myth of the poem' in which scholars accept an assertion that the poem has three significant moments of authorial authorization, which can be labelled A, B, and C.

To put it in other terms, the history of scholarship on *Piers Plowman* confronts the diversity of *Piers* manuscripts by, in part, multiplying the moments of authorial authorization. As a result, the problem of the manuscript diversity of *Piers* has regularly been accommodated within a perspective that sees each manuscript as failing to accurately represent an ideal version: the number of ideal (authoritative) versions was simply multiplied until the remaining manuscript variations could be more or less easily identified as (scribal) failures. In short, our response to *Piers Plowman* has almost universally accepted the notion that physical manuscripts or modern printed editions can indeed attempt to represent a single ideal version, even if we have needed to multiply the number of ideal versions in order to maintain that principle. My argument throughout this chapter, of course, attempts to suggest something quite different: Langland himself and the scribes involved in copying out the poem may have felt rather that *Piers Plowman* was always a moving target: a poem more or less constantly variable and under revision. Rather than 'publishing' a sequence of 'authorized' versions of *Piers Plowman*, Langland may have simply been an inveterate tinkerer, with never an idea that he should not be one.[26] Instead, Langland's Gothic perspective must have recognized that each reproduction of the poem *Piers Plowman* would always feature individual, local variations: his and his poem's scribes' tinkerings may function as successful Gothic elaborations without necessarily falling into a paradigm which must identify them either as authorized successes at accurate reproduction of the ideal or as mere failures.

One of the most specific consequences of recognizing the possibility that even Langland understands his poem as subject to what I have described as Gothic reproduction may well be to redefine our understanding of the poem's development. Implicit in our habit of identifying multiple moments of authorial authorization and publication is the notion of textual development: but Langland's tinkering need not have involved any such linear progress, and manuscripts that show A-text tendencies combined with C-text tendencies need not be seen as 'contaminated' or 'corrupted', although such derogatory terms continue to

---

[26] Compare Ralph Hanna III, *William Langland*. Authors of the Middle Ages 3 (Aldershot: Variorum, 1993), p. 10, who suggests that the poem may have undergone a 'process of constant revision' rather than specific, distinct moments of revision and publication.

be used in scholarly discussions. Notions of textual contamination, of course, depend explicitly upon a central belief in a kind of originary purity that copies (ideally) attempt to maintain. The controlling ideology of Gothic reproduction, however, can recognize a mixed version as an acceptable copy of a moving target original. It is important to recognize that I am not suggesting that attempting to trace linear developments in either Langland's ideas for the poem or in the development of the poem across the manuscript tradition is pointless; my argument is that the underlying meaning or significance of variation across manuscripts differs, according to whether the author or scribe perceives the object of copying to be an 'ideal' original version or a 'moving target' original version. The multiformity of Langland manuscripts is not in itself a problem (though it may well give us problems), but an expression of their essential adherence to the ideology of Gothic reproduction, as opposed to ideal reproduction.

And yet it remains important to also note that *Piers Plowman* articulates itself largely without a controlling or defining suite of paratextual strategies: even the name of the author, 'William Langland', is the result of modern scholarly reconstruction, from medieval evidence that is itself multivalent and subject to interpretation.[27] Various manuscript rubrics do seem to name the work 'liber de pet*rus* ploughman' or the like, but like the division into passus (the sections of the poem) and the titles or labels for individual passus, such titles vary from manuscript to manuscript.[28] Given the number of surviving manuscripts, and the likelihood that the author did himself produce multiple versions of the poem, it is difficult not to imagine that the poem was always intended for multiplication and Gothic reproduction, but the diversity of manuscripts may well have been supported or aided by the general lack of paratextual definition, as such a lack of definition would correspond to the 'moving target' nature of the reproducible text with a special appositeness. In other words, while Geoffrey of Monmouth and Marie de France apply their names as part of a text-defining paratextual strategy,

---

[27] See Benson, *Public Piers Plowman*, pp. 77–107, on 'the myth of the poet'.

[28] As Benson, *Public Piers Plowman*, p. 128 notes, 'Several *Piers* manuscripts have unique passus divisions and one C-text has a series of illustrations. Most have some form of annotation, with no program exactly like another.' Benson here discusses *Piers Plowman* as a 'multitext' which captures some of what I am here attempting, although from a somewhat different perspective.

even while anticipating Gothic reproduction, Langland's cryptic self-naming obscures authorial definition in a fashion that authorizes non-identical copies even more directly.

Given that possibility, it seems important to consider the quite different circumstances that surround *The Book of Margery Kempe*.[29] Kempe's lengthy spiritual autobiography (if such a designation is correct) has a quite complex paratextual apparatus: the book is separated into two separate books (of 89 and 10 chapters, respectively), plus two initial prefaces and a final appendix of Kempe's prayers. The two prefaces give a date of composition for Liber I in 1436, while the opening of Liber II dates its composition to 1438. The content of the two prefaces, remarkably, identifies the version of the book we have as a copy made (with the help of Kempe) from an earlier, nearly illegible version, 'neiþyr good Englysch ne Dewch, ne þe lettyr was not schapyn ne formyd as oþer lettres ben'.[30] The linguistic indeterminacy of the source, along with the cryptic nature of the characters, is surprisingly reminiscent of the pseudo-textual Vintry ampulla discussed above; the inaccessibility of the original version places Kempe's book solidly into the Gothic ideology of reproduction through the very imperfection of the original that is being reproduced. Indeed, the inaccessibility of Kempe's original might even recall Geoffrey of Monmouth. Though Kempe's scribe's sudden ability to read the malformed original is presented as deriving from a gift of God's grace, his reading still depended on Kempe, 'sche sum-tym helpyng where ony difficulte was': even with divine help, the original remained cryptic, at least in places, and its reproduction into the text we now read was accomplished in a fashion that advertises its contingency, authorized by Kempe herself as much as by its textual original.[31]

On the other hand, of course, the structure of the book, with its carefully labelled books and chapters and dates, gives *The Book of Margery Kempe* a well-articulated textual identity and historical position. Like *Piers Plowman*, however, it lacks a defining title, and the name of the author is almost entirely obscured, her surname appearing only once, buried in the middle of Liber II, chapter 9.[32] Unlike *Piers Plowman*,

---

[29] Meech, ed., *The Book of Margery Kempe*. Benson, *Public Piers Plowman*, pp. 129–31, also compares Langland to Kempe, although again with a somewhat different perspective than I take here.

[30] Meech, ed., *Book of Margery Kempe*, p. 4.

[31] Meech, ed., *Book of Margery Kempe*, p. 5.

[32] Meech, ed., *Book of Margery Kempe*, p. 243.

Kempe's book never achieved any sort of widespread distribution, as far as we can tell, with only a single manuscript surviving to the present, alongside some exceedingly brief early printed extracts. But, of course, not every book whose author anticipates widespread publication receives it, and it is unlikely that the failure of *The Book of Margery Kempe* to be widely copied resulted from her coyness about her name and the book's lack of an explicit title. What is remarkable is how, in a book modern readers often praise or condemn for its very idiosyncrasies, Kempe's prefaces and other paratextual materials place her book into the mainstream of Gothic literature, with well-defined boundaries, an author's name and precise historical position to give context, and a written source explicitly described as failing to underwrite the copy or copies it generates.

The examples of the *Pearl*-poet, Langland (if that is his real name), and Margery Kempe serve to remind us that the central features of Gothic reproduction, dominant as it seemingly was, nevertheless still allowed room for variation, including even some productions that seem dissociated entirely from the logic of textual reproduction, in terms of both textual uniqueness and lack of paratextual definition. Just as a reading of Anglo-Saxon textual culture reminded us of the necessity of reading and seeing to determine whether a particular work was composed, produced, or reproduced under the paradigm of production or reproduction, we must do the same with works written and disseminated during the Gothic era. The relative cultural prominence of the domains of 'production' and 'reproduction' seems to have reversed during the transition between the Anglo-Saxon and Gothic periods, but both paradigms remained available. Our understanding of individual works must always attend to how those works are situated within these competing paradigms.

Producing The Canterbury Tales

The Riverside Chaucer, the standard scholarly edition of the poet's works, suggests 'For reasons unknown, Chaucer left *The Canterbury Tales* incomplete and without final revision.'[33] In the rubric at the head of the Hengwrt manuscript, in the colophon at the end of Ellesmere, and in the

---

[33] Benson, ed., *The Riverside Chaucer*, p. 5.

Retraction (also preserved in Ellesmere; the end of the Hengwrt manuscript is missing), the great work is consistently called 'the tales of caunterbury' and our own preferred title stands in direct conflict with this early testimony.[34] Since the *Tales* exemplify a quite complex paratextuality, in which Geoffrey Chaucer's name, the title of the overall work, and the names and textual boundaries of the various tale-tellers' texts are all carefully delineated through both prefaces and rubrics (and in both Ellesmere and Hengwrt, running heads at the tops of pages), our preference for our own modern title must reflect an assumption that the fidelity we owe to Chaucer's text need not apply so fully to paratextual features, including even the title. Our mode of reading, receiving, and reproducing texts takes the text/paratext split very seriously indeed, and yet Chaucer (especially in the *Tales*) is surely as conscious of the textual play involved with his work's paratexts as Marie de France showed herself to be in her playful contesting of her own *lais'* titles.

Both of these Gothic authors, from nearly opposite ends of the Gothic period, appear to be taking the text/paratext split as part of their own literary materials, part of what they both work with and respond to, as they negotiate the ideological content of Gothic reproduction in relation to their own compositions. To the degree that the apparent incompleteness and lack of consistent ordering of *The Canterbury Tales* correspond to what I have described as the 'moving target' nature of the Gothic source or original, *The Canterbury Tales* succeeds brilliantly at expressing and using its own status as a product of Gothic reproduction, rather than implicitly failing at either completeness or revision. Even if both Hengwrt and Ellesmere were produced after Chaucer's death, their differences manifest the moving target nature of what they are copying: in the absence of an actual act of collation, both Ellesmere and Hengwrt are very good copies of *The Canterbury Tales* indeed, and modern editors still have difficulty choosing which manuscript or text is better for their purposes. But further, the nature of the moving target original removes any need to associate either ordering of the *Tales* with an evolving intention on Chaucer's part. Medieval authors, scribes, and

---

[34] See the facsimiles of Hengwrt and Ellesmere: *The Ellesmere Manuscript of Chaucer's Canterbury Tales: A Working Facsimile*, Introduction by Ralph Hanna III (Cambridge: D. S. Brewer, 1989) and Paul G. Ruggiers, ed., *The Canterbury Tales: A Facsimile and Transcription of the Hengwrt Manuscript, with Variants from the Hengwrt Manuscript* (Norman, OK: University of Oklahoma Press, 1979).

readers, inhabiting the ideology of Gothic moving target reproduction from the inside, swam where we are sometimes afraid of drowning.

And they must have often needed to swim indeed. Of the eighty-two or eighty-three complete or fragmentary manuscripts of the *Tales*, fifty-five 'appear to have been intended as complete texts', whatever that might mean in relation to the *Tales*.[35] Fully twenty-five of those fifty-five include the anonymous, non-Chaucerian, 902-line romance now known as *Gamelyn*, almost always after the unfinished or incomplete *Cook's Tale*.[36] Five manuscripts include John Lydgate's *Siege of Thebes*, which includes a prologue in which Lydgate joins the pilgrimage at Canterbury and tells his tale on the return journey towards London.[37] One of these Lydgate manuscripts, Oxford, Christ Church College 152, includes a version of Hoccleve's poem *Item de Beata Virgine* as the *Plowman's Tale*.[38] One manuscript, Northumberland MS 455, includes a lengthy and amusing account of the pilgrims' sojourn in Canterbury (*The Canterbury Interlude*) as well as a second tale offered up by the Merchant, *The Tale of Beryn*.[39] A substantial number of fifteenth-century readers would have known *The Tales of Caunterbury* in a form very different indeed from what we call *The Canterbury Tales*.

Our habitual excision of these other texts from *The Canterbury Tales*, of course, depends upon a concept of authorial authorization based in the notion of an ideal text, rather than a moving target. Operating without that notion, medieval scribes and authors could envision a version of *The Tales of Caunterbury* that was substantially different from any imagined by Chaucer himself, with varying degrees of explicitness about the Chaucerian and non-Chaucerian parts. It is certainly possible to read the composition of non-Chaucerian links and prologues as an effort to remedy the 'aesthetic embarrassment' of the work's incompleteness,[40] but the same motive cannot really account for the inclusion of *Gamelyn*, or Lydgate's *Siege of Thebes*, or *Beryn*, or the Hocclevian *Plowman's Tale*. These additions go beyond the work of making the incomplete complete,

---

[35] Benson, ed., *The Riverside Chaucer*, p. 1118.
[36] John M. Bowers, ed., *The Canterbury Tales: Fifteenth-Century Continuations and Additions* (Kalamazoo, MI: Medieval Institute Publications, 1992), p. 33.
[37] Bowers, ed., *Continuations*, p. 12.
[38] Bowers, ed., *Continuations*, p. 24.
[39] Bowers, ed., *Continuations*, pp. 55–196.
[40] Bowers, ed., *Continuations*, p. 3.

as they supplement Chaucer's work with something entirely new, and yet, just about as often as not, medieval manuscripts include one or more of these additions. To the degree that Lydgate's long work and the Beryn-poet's unique additions involve the return trip from Canterbury to Southwark, these additions sometimes seem, in fact, to run counter to what we can determine about Chaucer's intention, which appears to have been to end the text with the arrival at Canterbury. Our modern tendency to see the incompleteness of *The Canterbury Tales* as a failure of some sort has caused us to interpret 'spurious' links and continuations as responding to that particular failure, but such a perspective cannot really account for some of the additions' patent lack of association between 'completeness' and any intention of Chaucer's. The medieval recognition—employed and even played with by Chaucer, I would argue—that *The Tales of Caunterbury* had only a 'moving target' original form opened the door for later poets' and scribes' own unique contributions to be incorporated into later reproductions of that 'original'. If *The Canterbury Tales* is our title for the work as we imagine it as subject to Chaucer's final controlling intention, we must recognize that the Gothic *Tales of Caunterbury* operated by a different logic, according to which local variations were allowable and even valued. We might think, for example, that the Northumberland manuscript, with *The Canterbury Interlude* and *The Tale of Beryn*, is not a good manuscript of *The Canterbury Tales*, but it seems likely to me to be a fine example indeed of *The Tales of Caunterbury*.

Gothic mechanical reproduction

In contrast to the handwritten manuscripts of the Gothic middle ages, where precise, perfect, mechanical reproduction was an impossible ideal, the literally mechanical technology of mould-based metallic reproduction might be taken to suggest that secular and religious pilgrim badges should exemplify the reproductive, duplicative aspects of the Gothic aesthetic at the expense of variation or individuation. Yet even mechanically produced pilgrim badges seem to have been manufactured under the ideological paradigm of 'moving target' Gothic reproduction, and a closer look at pilgrim badges can serve both to suggest again that Gothic reproduction is a component of the Gothic visual economy (rather than just a component of Gothic textuality) and to remind us that the link between mechanical reproduction and the notion of an 'ideal' or 'perfect' original is itself an ideological linkage, not a necessary one. It is especially useful to consider how pilgrim badges were used to visually represent another particular aspect of Gothic visual culture, that of Gothic architecture.

Surely the most remarkable pilgrim badge to survive from the middle ages is the immense badge which Spencer associates with Canterbury's 'Our Lady Undercroft' (Spencer no. 136; Figure 3).[41] A full fourteen centimetres tall, two pins were apparently necessary for attaching this badge to the clothing, but the presence of such pins does suggest that it was intended to be worn, just as many smaller badges were. Much of the height of this badge, of course, derives not from the four figures, but from the manifestly Gothic architectural surround in which those figures are placed. Surviving examples of this badge are rare, but it does seem to be the case that the Gothic tracery was intended to be openwork, although the production process was not without its flaws, resulting in the filling in of much of the tracery in this particular example. The open tracery, however, takes on additional significance given Spencer's observation that the badge 'was also given six clips . . . for the attachment of a backing', although Spencer does not further discuss the backing.[42] The backing does not survive to the present, of course, because the muddy, anaerobic conditions that preserved the badge itself did not favour the survival of the backing material, which was probably vellum, paper, or cloth.

The failure of the backing material to survive, however, does not leave us entirely in the dark: the combination of the metallic openwork and backing does in its own way insist upon the importance of the backing material's visibility. In the simplest imaginable case, the pale natural surface of a vellum or paper backing would have highlighted the openwork, but the architectural context surely suggests that a coloured background was envisioned by the maker and presumably supplied to the badge before purchase: the visual effect of the badge replicated some of the effect of a Gothic stained-glass window. This possibility is almost certainly confirmed by the survival of badges (often but not always

[41] Spencer, *Pilgrim Souvenirs*, no. 136, pp. 129–33.
[42] Spencer, *Pilgrim Souvenirs*, p. 131; my ellipsis.

FIG 3 Our Lady Undercroft (Canterbury) badge, showing Gothic architectural surround.

Image courtesy of The Museum of London.

including clips for the attachment of a backing) that seem to represent stained-glass windows in their own right, including circular rose windows (see Figure 4).[43] In such examples, there seems to be no reason to doubt that coloured backing materials would have been attached, though one doubts that they could possibly have been coloured with the level of detail seen in actual surviving windows:[44] even in the context of mechanical reproduction of the metallic portions of these badges, the backing materials were unlikely to function as representations in a fashion to suggest that absolute fidelity to the original (the stained glass in these cases) could have been intended. Further, the unlikelihood of a truly accurate depiction of medieval stained glass in these badges suggests the possibility that such badges might well have varied in colour one from another, in a very Gothic kind of individuation amidst reproduction. Even if we imagine truly accurate reproduction of stained-glass designs, two Gothic windows placed next to one another would generally have had the same general outline and tracery, but differed in their images (another kind of variation within repetition) and two badges from the same mould might reflect two different actual windows. The surviving badges with traces of polychrome paint in the French corpus published by Denis Bruna remind us of another mode in which these mechanically produced badges were probably individuated, rather than being manufactured with identicalness as a goal.[45] While we usually see only the metal portions of these badges, due to the nature of their survival, a

[43] Without attempting a full list, openwork badges with clear Gothic architectural elements are common in the published collections of badges from the low countries in H. J. E. van Beuningen and A. M. Koldeweij, *Heilig en Profaan: 1000 Laatmiddeleeuwse Insignes uit de Collectie H. J. E. van Beuningen*, Rotterdam Papers VIII (Cothen: Stichting Middeleeuwse Religieuze en Profane Insignes, 1993) and H. J. E. van Beuningen, A. M. Koldeweij, and D. Kicken, *Heilig en Profaan 2: 1200 Laatmiddeleeuwse Insignes uit Openbare en Particuliere Collecties*, Rotterdam Papers XII (Cothen: Stichting Middeleeuwse Religieuze en Profane Insignes, 2001). Illustration numbers are consecutive across these two volumes, and especially clear examples of Gothic architectural openwork badges include *HP*1, nos. 49, 120, 127, 164, 190, 233–8, 273–4, 289, 297, 336, 361, 414, 416, 525, and *HP*2 nos. 1188, 1191, 1202, 1275, 1342, 1352, 1354–62, 1371–7, 2023–9, with this last group explicitly compared to cathedral rose windows in van Beuningen, Koldeweij, and Kicken, *Heilig en Profaan* 2, p. 452.

[44] One should, however, note the unique survival of a polychrome painted image (upon a papery surface) within an Aachen diptych found in 2000 and shown in van Beuningen, Koldeweij, and Kicken, *Heilig en Profaan* 2, no. 1370, p. 326.

[45] See Denis Bruna, *Enseignes de Pèlerinage et Enseignes Profanes* (Paris: Éditions de la Réunion des musées nationaux, 1996), colour plates, pp. 36–8.

variety of considerations encourage us to see them in context as featuring variation within repetition, rather than being identical reproductions of an ideal original.

We might have reached a similar conclusion, however, from a very different source, *The Canterbury Interlude* written by the Beryn-poet and surviving uniquely, as discussed above, in the Northumberland manuscript of Chaucer's *Tales*. In the following passage, the pilgrims have arrived at Canterbury, and so they set about acquiring their souvenirs:

> Then, as manere and custome is, signes there they boughte,
> For men of contre shuld know whom they had soughte.
> Ech man set his sylver in such thing as they liked.
> And in the meenwhile, the Miller had i-piked
> His bosom ful of signes of Caunterbury broches,
> Huch the Pardoner and he pryvely in hir pouches
> They put hem afterward, that noon of hem it wist,

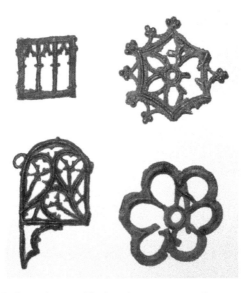

FIG 4   Four Gothic architectural badges, from a private collection. The lower two badges were found in Nieuwlande, NL; the other two badges' find spots are unrecorded. Image © Thomas A. Bredehoft.

> Save the Sompnour seid somwhat and seyd to hem, 'List,
> Halff part!' quod he pryvely, rownyng on hir ere.[46]

The Pardoner, we know from *The General Prologue*, already has a verni-cle from Rome 'sowed upon his cappe',[47] and *The Canterbury Interlude* suggests that souvenirs from both Rome and Canterbury supposedly served to let 'men of contre' know just where pilgrims have travelled to—whether the badges have been purchased legitimately or stolen. The echo of the Pardoner's larceny in relation to relics is probably inten-tional on the Beryn-poet's part, and the signifying power of the badge-signs displayed by pilgrims is certainly also put into question here. After all, the Miller, Pardoner, and Summoner presumably steal more than they can use themselves: the mass reproduction of the badges allows a proliferation of images that function as signs, but the meaning of those signs as certification of an actual pilgrimage is undermined by their theft and the illicit circulation of such signs that presumably results. *The Canterbury Interlude* effectively expresses that the pictures of Becket or his shrine (or, indeed, the Our Lady Undercroft) which these badges probably show are culturally and ideally intended to certify whom these pilgrims 'had soughte', but the theft simultaneously acknowledges the failure of that representation, because a stolen sign surely cannot sig-nify authentically. The value of these signs is social, then, not necessar-ily reliant on even the sanctity of Becket himself as a transcendental signifier, but rather certified by a social acceptance of their meaning. The function of badges as signs ideally operates according to a reliable Saussurian signifier–signified relationship, but the theft of the badges reminds us that what these signs signify cannot be stable: it is also a moving target.

In somewhat different terms, the badge scene in *The Canterbury Interlude* also makes it clear that badges are offered in a variety of mass-produced designs so that individual pilgrims can choose examples that appeal to their own personal tastes, however they manage to acquire them: 'Ech man set his sylver in such thing as they liked.' Certainly, the published corpora of surviving badges often show very many designs that are both very similar and characterized by seemingly endless

---

[46] *Canterbury Interlude*, ll. 171–9; I cite this poem from Bowers, ed., *Continuations*.

[47] *Canterbury Tales*, fragment I, l. 685.

variation. It is difficult not to conclude that badges were both individually mass produced (each design mass produced) *and* produced in profusion, either with multiple designs produced to attract various purchasers, or with each badge individuated (with paint or different backing colours). To the degree that the function of badges as 'signes' often involved a visual association with the objects of the pilgrimage (the Becket shrine or head reliquary, Mary's tunic at Aachen, the miraculous three hosts at Wilsnack, or specific stained-glass windows), they functioned representationally. But the visual variety of such signs did not in itself undermine their value as representations, because they made (and needed) no claims of unique representational precision. That is, a badge depicting the Becket head-reliquary was understood to look like the head-reliquary, but it did not need to be, and was not expected to be, identical to other such badges: the original authorized a variety of visual representations without generating a hierarchy of value based upon an assessment of their accuracy or faithfulness—here, too, the 'original' is a kind of moving target that authorizes reproductions that vary from one another. Pilgrim badge signs operated in what must have been a widespread and familiar visual economy across Europe, and the Miller's and Pardoner's theft of badges exemplifies their eagerness to participate in this visual economy, even while they subvert the workings of the money economy that made it possible. But the visual economy of pilgrim (and secular) badges was itself quite literally made possible by the technologies of reproduction and the ideology of reproduction that made those technologies possible. The technology of mechanical production may well invoke the logic of the copy, in which copies always fail to reproduce their original accurately, but in the world of Gothic reproduction, that failure could well be productive and valuable: the local variation that generated individual character and meanings.

Chaucer's House of Fame

At the opening of *The House of Fame*, Chaucer's narrator (named 'Geffrey' at line 749) dreams of 'a temple ymad of glas', and it is difficult not to envision a grand Gothic church or cathedral with rank upon rank of stained-glass windows.[48] Within this temple of glass, the dreamer encounters an inscribed brass plaque, which begins as follows:

> I wol now synge, yif I kan,
> The armes and also the man.[49]

The opening of Vergil's *Aeneid* is here translated into Chaucerian English, complete with a caveat of translatorial inadequacy, and without attempting a full reading of *The House of Fame*, I hope to suggest here that Chaucer's thematizing of translation in this poem expresses his investment in characteristic Gothic concerns as clearly as did the translational games of Geoffrey of Monmouth or Marie de France in the twelfth century. Indeed, as with Will's dreams in *Piers Plowman* or Kempe's visions in *The Book of Margery Kempe*, Chaucer's use of the dream vision genre itself invokes an original that is utterly inaccessible to the reading audience, even less accessible than Monmouth's British book or de France's linguistically indeterminate *lais*.

After reading the plaque, Chaucer's narrator says 'And tho began the story anoon', and what follows is a lengthy description of what he sees within the temple, 'peynted on the wal' or 'graven eke withal'.[50] Notably, definition 8 of 'story' in the *Oxford English Dictionary* is 'A painting or sculpture representing a historical subject. Hence, any work of pictorial or sculptural art containing figures', and this definition is likely to be the operative one here in *The House of Fame*: the story the dreamer sees is literally a series of images. The particular story, of course, is Vergil's *Aeneid*, as announced by the plaque, though (again) with some characteristic Chaucerian interventions, such as a greatly expanded lament from Dido.[51] In the absence of manuscript illustrations, modern readers have often been uncertain about whether the images Geffrey describes are to be understood as wall paintings or stained-glass windows, though wall paintings seem to be envisioned in the standard interpretation.[52] It is important, however, to recognize the ways in which the *Aeneid* passage

---

[48] *House of Fame*, l. 120.
[49] *House of Fame*, ll. 143–4.
[50] *House of Fame*, ll. 149, 211–12.
[51] See the explanatory note to line 314 in Benson, ed., *The Riverside Chaucer*, p. 980.
[52] See, e.g., Benson, ed., *The Riverside Chaucer*, p. 347, where, in the headnote to the poem, John M. Fyler suggests wall painting and does not even hint at the possibility of stained glass.

of *The House of Fame* is more than an extended exercise of *ekphrasis*, the literary description of a work of art; rather, we have here a Chaucerian demonstration of translation as a Gothic phenomenon, complete with a moving target original. As such, it seems to me that the images must surely be best seen as stained glass.

My argument throughout this chapter has been that the Gothic mode of reproduction was one in which the logic of the copy dominated, but with a different dynamic than it has for us. We see the failure of copies to match their targeted sources or originals as indeed being a matter of failure, while Gothic reproduction, if my argument is correct, treats the failure of Gothic reproductions as an occasion or opportunity for local, individual variation among the resultant copies, due to an underlying conception of the original as a moving target, inherently inaccessible or inescapably multiform. The opening of Geffrey's dream in *The House of Fame*, then, presents us with two 'translations' of Vergil's *Aeneid* in the temple, in the form of the linguistic translation on the brass plaque and the series of graphic depictions that appear on the walls or windows. It hardly needs to be noted that the 'story' depicted on the walls or windows does not begin with a translation of 'Arma virumque cano': the presence of two (partial) translations of *The Aeneid* naturally enough results in two somewhat different stories here. The linguistic translation and the visual representations (as Chaucer transcribes them back into words) take two different forms, both based in the same original but necessarily differing from one another, perfectly in line with what I have described as characterizing Gothic reproduction. But to the degree that the 'original' is ideally visible behind the translation, the Chaucerian or Gothic translation, I believe, is more like stained glass than like a wall painting. Stained glass, by its very nature, allows the light to pass through it, and the light both shines through and is filtered or altered during the passage in a way that can surely be described as translation. Our understanding of the 'story' seen by the dreamer as stained glass helps clarify the poem's investment in and interrogation of Gothic representation and its relation to the distant or inaccessible original.

Regardless, once Geffrey the dreamer reaches the end of the 'story', his first thought is to wonder who had made the images he had been looking upon, before even wondering what country he might be in.[53] Again, the

---

[53] *House of Fame*, ll. 464–5.

close association between explicit translation and the idea of an identifiable author is clear, even if Geffrey's desire to learn the artist's name is here doomed. Likewise, instead of finding himself in an identifiable land or country, upon exiting the temple he finds himself in a vast desert of sand, from which he is plucked by a golden eagle and taken up into the air to visit the House of Fame. Along the way, the eagle explains that the visit to the House of Fame is Geffrey's reward for serving Cupid. At the House, the eagle explains, Geffrey will see all human sounds and speeches (including tidings of love in particular) arriving and mixing, each speech looking just like the person who spoke it. This imagery, of course, presents a second twist on the notion of duplication and accurate representation, though the eagle, of course, claims that the representations are indeed accurate:

> Whan any speche ycomen ys
> Up to the paleys, anon-ryght
> Hyt wexeth lyk the same wight
> Which that the word in erthe spak,
> Be hyt clothed red or blak;
> And hath so verray hys lyknesse
> That spak the word, that thou wilt gesse
> That it the same body be,
> Man or woman, he or she,
> And ys not this a wonder thyng?[54]

'Yis' answers Geffrey in the next line, 'by heven kyng!', reminding us that the dream of perfect reproduction is indeed impossible in the Gothic world without the kind of divine or sacred sanction described above in the case of Becket's blood. That these embodied speeches are, as the eagle's earlier scientific discourse admits, nothing more than 'air ybroke' must surely acknowledge even these representations' subjectivity to the logic of the copy: the eagle has temporarily given in to the dream of perfect representation, even as he brings Geffrey right to the castle of Fame herself.[55] And, indeed, after a time spent in Fame's castle, where Geffrey sees the goddess's capricious nature at first hand, he retreats to another dwelling in hopes of 'Somme newe tydynges for to lere'.[56] But what he sees instead is that

---

[54] *House of Fame*, ll. 1074–83
[55] *House of Fame*, l. 770.
[56] *House of Fame*, l. 1886.

> Whan oon had herd a thyng, ywis,
> He com forth ryght to another wight,
> And gan him to tellen anon-ryght
> The same that to him was told,
> Or hyt a furlong way was old,
> But gan somwhat for to eche
> To this tydynge in this speche
> More than it ever was.[57]

The ever-increasing size of the tidings here, complicated by the way in which the people Geffrey sees in this structure are themselves other tidings taking the shapes of those who spoke them back on earth, gives the scene a dreamlike complexity, even as it reasserts the impossibility of an accurate translation or transmission of text. Indeed, the tidings get blown up with air until they fly up and out through windows and crevices, whether true or false, or a combination of the two. Any hope the author or speaker of a particular tiding might have of controlling its size or content is illusory: the tidings have only moving target originals. The house these inflated tidings escape from, always described in criticism of the poem as the House of Rumor (though never so identified in the poem) is surely best understood as a windmill, the very original, perhaps, of the proverbial rumour mill, ceaselessly turned by the power of wind or 'air ybroke'.[58]

Throughout the poem, then, Chaucer repeatedly assesses the accuracy of textual, linguistic, and visual representations, all of which, in the end, are represented as failing, utterly in agreement with the logic of the copy, which insists that all representations fail. But for Chaucer, as for the Gothic period in general, that necessary failure is an opportunity for play and productivity, and here Chaucer takes its nature as his text, linking it to the capricious nature of fame in a new and thoroughly Gothic fashion. At the very end of the poem, the dreamer says that he saw the approach of

> a man
> Whiche that y nat ne kan

---

[57] *House of Fame*, ll. 2060–7.
[58] The name 'House of Rumor' is taken as needing no explanation in Benson, ed., *Riverside Chaucer*, p. 989, explanatory note to ll. 1925–85.

But he semed for to be
A man of gret auctoritee.[59]

As with so many things in Chaucer, the identity of this figure has long been a matter of scholarly debate, but it seems to me that the vision here must end with Chaucer facing himself (although he does not appear to recognize himself). Whoever it is, of course, appears in the form of a 'tydynge' from below, appearing in the guise of its author: if we read the 'man of gret auctoritee' as Chaucer, the tiding in question, one would have to imagine, is the present poem itself. The end of *House of Fame*, which has so often seemed fragmentary or incomplete, reflects instead the recursive funhouse mirror-upon-mirror magnifying multiplication that ought to result if Chaucer approaches this tiding, which (according to the rules described earlier in the poem) ought to speak itself to whomever it meets. The reproduction of the poem is here made equivalent to the reproduction of the author, who will, no doubt, pass the poem along in an enlarged and improved form, blowing it up along with his own fame; indeed, with such an interpretation in mind, one cannot help but think of Langland's seeming inability to keep from expanding or improving upon the text of *Piers Plowman* each time he re-encounters it. If my previous account of the Gothic aesthetic is correct, in that it plays upon the tension between identical repetition and the necessary variation that makes meaning from each unique iteration, the final scene of the poem, in which the poet-narrator Geffrey faces himself, operates effectively on that very tension, writing into its own text the inability of the author to grant the text a stable original form that can escape the ideological consequences of being a moving target. The recursive ending of *House of Fame*, like the rest of the poem, is built upon the Gothic ideology of 'moving target' visual and textual reproduction.

Our modern mode of articulating the logic of the copy is grounded in the notion that representations necessarily fail to represent accurately, but in the Gothic mode I have attempted to describe in this chapter, the 'moving target' nature of Gothic originals is an occasion for productive textual, visual, and translational *variance*, rather than problematic failure. Rather than understanding the impossibility of an equation

---

[59] *House of Fame*, ll. 2155–8. Editors generally insert 'nevene' into line 2156 for metrical reasons, but I leave it out here, as in the manuscripts, while also restoring final '-e' to 'Whiche', as that seems to be all that is needed to make the line metrically acceptable.

between original and copy as a problem, Gothic reproduction understands the irreducible difference between original and copy as an opportunity: in a very real sense, much Gothic literature is literally written
upon Derrida's *supplément*, that irreducible, unbridgeable gap between
a representation and what it supposedly represents, although perhaps in
a fashion that Derrida himself does not seem to imagine. From the thematizing of translation in Geoffrey of Monmouth and Marie de France
in the twelfth century to the dream visions of Chaucer, Langland, and
even the *Pearl*-poet in the fourteenth, the most 'literary' authors of the
period problematize and play with the idea of the original as an authorizing source, just as Margery Kempe plays the authority of her own
experience off against the unreadability of her book's first manuscript.
But the nature of the moving target Gothic source is to be productive of
literature, a source of possibility and play, rather than an ideological
failure to be guarded against.

Interlude 2

Gothic to Print

My discussion above of the Our Lady Undercroft badge from Canterbury (Figure 3) raised the possibility that openwork badges, with or without typical Gothic architectural tracery, were very often likely to have been fitted with a colourful backing of paper or vellum, attached either by means of clips or possibly even by thread or glue. Among the extensive collections of badges published by Dutch collector H. J. E. van Beuningen and his collaborators, the largest and most interesting grouping of such openwork badges is surely the series of badges associated with the Aachen pilgrimage.[1] These badges often show Mary's tunic, an especially precious relic held at Aachen and seen there by vast numbers of pilgrims. Indeed, the crowds at the septennial exhibition of the Aachen relics were so large that Aachen badges often included tiny mirrors, apparently to allow pilgrims to catch an image of the relics in their mirrors, even if the press of the crowds prohibited them from seeing the relics directly with their eyes.

I think it is probably fair to say that, given the apparent size of the crowds, such badges must have been produced by the thousands, and the degree of openwork on many of these badges is quite remarkable. The likelihood that the backings of these badges were coloured raises the question of exactly how the production of so many complex backing

---

[1] Specifically, see badges *HP1*, nos. 416–25, 428–32 and *HP2*, nos. 1340–55.

pieces was accomplished. One possibility, of course, is handwork: a kind of prototypically Gothic mode of hand-individuation that supplemented the mechanical reproduction of the metal portions of the badges to express the Gothic variation-within-repetition aesthetic with special precision. But it is at least possible to imagine that some or all of these coloured backings were printed: woodcut technology existed before the invention of movable type itself, and early woodblock prints include some which were apparently intended as pilgrim souvenirs. Indeed, woodcut technology might have enabled especially clear depictions of stained glass in architectural badges. Regardless, when we recall that Gutenberg himself attempted to mass-produce badges for the Aachen festival season (although not immune from disputes with his partners over which year would see the relics displayed[2]), the possibility that Gutenberg was familiar with both metallurgical and printing aspects of badge production might well account for the ensuing invention of movable-type printing. Indeed, the invention of printing begins to seem almost overdetermined, the very culmination of the Gothic mode of imagining reproduction.

[2] See the convenient summary of the Strasbourg documents in Otto W. Fuhrmann, *Gutenberg and the Strasbourg Documents of 1439: An Interpretation* (New York: Press of the Woolly Whale, 1940), pp. 49–50.

| 3 |

Typographic Print Reproduction

To a surprising degree, printed books throughout the incunabula period remained thoroughly Gothic productions: although printing rubrications in red was attempted occasionally even from the very start, the norm throughout the fifteenth century was for printed books to receive (or to be intended to receive) hand-applied rubrication.[1] In practice, the hand-rubrication of fifteenth-century printed books resulted in the classic Gothic dynamic of individual unique variation within more or less identical reproduction. In one sense, the continuing presence of handwork within incunabula expresses the degree to which early printed books were also simultaneously manuscripts, but more certainly, the dynamic of variation-within-reproduction expresses the essential Gothicism of the incunabula period. A transition period of some fifty or seventy years was seemingly needed to move the production of printed books fully within the paradigm of printing and (non-Gothic) modern print reproduction, in which the ideological notion that printed texts do indeed have an ideal form truly took hold.

[1] On rubrication in fifteenth-century printed books, see the fine essay by Margaret M. Smith, 'Red as a Textual Element during the Transition from Manuscript to Print', in Orietta Da Rold and Elaine Treharne, eds., *Textual Cultures: Cultural Texts* (Cambridge: D. S. Brewer, 2010), pp. 187–200.

This chapter will attempt to survey the nature of that transition to the ideological paradigm of print, where the mediacy of print is understood by both book-makers and authors as resulting in a particular kind of failure, in part (at least at the start) because the printed text necessarily fails to be a manuscript. In short, in the full-blown print paradigm, the immediate visual uniformity of typography announces the visible text's status as a reproduction of something that is, by contrast, invisible or virtual: an underlying original that is not, itself, a printed text, and that is not present. Further, the chapter will trace two powerful responses to the ways in which print positions an ideal or virtual original as the locus of authority for printed works. On the one hand, book-makers and authors attempt to respond to the ideological failures of print by producing what I will call 'editions', which work to announce or articulate their authority and value by deploying a variety of (increasingly conventionalized) paratexts. Where paratexts (in Anglo-Saxon and Gothic contexts) were previously used to situate and define a work within the particular mode of medial, textual reproduction as opposed to unique production, under the print paradigm, where reproduction is both foundational and understood, paratexts quickly became recontextualized as a kind of response to or bulwark against the failures of print reproduction. Alternatively, since at least the nineteenth century, book-makers have sometimes responded to the failures of print by producing facsimiles, which explicitly try to make the underlying authoritative original directly visible to readers. It hardly needs to be noted, I think, that both strategies are sometimes employed. Before discussing editions and facsimiles in detail, however, it is useful to consider a pair of examples from opposite ends of the print tradition in order to see just how the print paradigm works, as well as the degree to which it has remained surprisingly stable for over five centuries.

The books that readers don't see

Douglas A. Anderson's 'Note on the Text' of *The Lord of the Rings* offers a remarkable view of both textual scholarship and the kinds of sources of error which are possible in the late twentieth-century printed text:

In the production of this first volume [of *The Lord of the Rings*], Tolkien experienced what became for him a continual problem: printer's errors and compositor's mistakes, including well-intentioned 'corrections' of his sometimes idiosyncratic usage. These 'corrections' include the altering of *dwarves* to *dwarfs*, *elvish* to *elfish*, *further* to *farther*, *nasturtians* to *nasturtiums*, *try and say* to *try to say* and ('worst of all' to Tolkien) *elven* to *elfin*.[2]

Precisely because it has been reproduced and reprinted in so many formats and forms, *The Lord of the Rings* has been (until recently, one hopes) notoriously riddled with minor textual inconsistencies and errors, and it seems likely that even Tolkien himself was either occasionally inconsistent or 'had failed to keep his notes in order' as he oversaw various revisions, editions, and printings.[3] What, then, does one do, unless one is fortunate enough to have a copy one trusts before one's eyes?

Most readers, I suspect, may not even notice these types of error or inconsistency, unless they become egregious, although the typesetters and compositors of Tolkien's works have themselves been readers, in their turn, and their actions can guide us towards an understanding of how readers read what they see. Specifically, all of the 'corrections' attributed to printers and compositors in the quotation above derive from an assumption made by those readers about a perceived clash between what they presumably saw before them in the setting copy and what they believed the printed text (for which they bore some responsibility) should look like. In short, these readers anticipated that the printed text should be a correct text, although Tolkien's idiosyncrasies and stylistic choices in fact generated a second standard of correctness that readers might apply: typesetters often simply applied one standard of correctness that should perhaps have been superseded by the author's intended standards. Such an understanding of the typesetters' changes, of course, means that the actions of both the typesetters and compositors *and* the textual scholars (including even Tolkien himself, in the case of his own corrections and revisions) proceed from exactly the same principles: perceived inaccuracies or inconsistencies in the text being read are understood (that is, read or interpreted) as failing to correspond to the

---

[2] Douglas A. Anderson, 'Note on the Text', in J. R. R. Tolkien, *The Lord of the Rings* (Boston: Houghton Mifflin, 2004), pp. xi–xvii, at p. xi.
[3] Anderson, 'Note on the Text', p. xii.

'correct' version of the text. Further, the active modification of the text to bring it more in line with the imagined correct version of the text is understood as an acceptable, even desirable, textual intervention, because the imagined correct version is what the printed version ought to reproduce.

It is important to acknowledge that, from such a perspective, it is not at all necessary for a 'correct' version of the text to have ever existed in reality: the imaginary or ideal existence of a 'correct' text is all that is required to justify the making of these kinds of corrections to a text, whether one is an editor, compositor, author, or textual scholar. To put the issues in slightly different terms, the imagined 'correct' text is understood as being characterized by authorial consistency; it is imagined by readers to be coherent by the operation of what Michel Foucault describes as the 'author function'. When faced with inconsistency or incoherence in the received or visible text, readers more or less automatically distinguish what they see from what they imagine: the visible text may be flawed, but the imagined text is unified, whole, and consistent—in a word, it is ideal, as only things in the world of ideas can be. The operation of this 'author function', while not limited to the print era, is very much a prototypical mode of reading within the print paradigm. As such, its consequences are of real interest; most significant for my argument is the way that this mode of reading always treats the printed (and even pre-printed) text as an imperfect (physical) representation of an ideal (imagined) text.

It is important to recognize that this mode of reading through the notion of a 'correct' original version is not a feature of the 'late age of print', but has characterized print virtually from the beginning. A well-known passage from the 'Prohemye' to Caxton's second edition of *The Canterbury Tales* describes the frustration of a reader of Chaucer's great work in terms remarkably reminiscent of Anderson's account of literally unauthorized features of *The Lord of the Rings*. Caxton writes

> I did do enprynte a certayne nombre of them [first edition copies of the *Tales*]/ whyche anon were sold to many and dyuerse gentyl men/ of whome one gentylman cam to me/ and said that this book was not accordyng in many places vnto the book that Gefferey chaucer had made/ To whom I answerd that I had made it accordyng to my copye/ and by me was nothyng added ne mynusshyd/ Thenne he sayd he knewe a book whyche hys fader had and moche louyd/ that was very

> trewe/ and accordyng to hys owen first book by hym made/ and sayd
> more yf I wold enprynte it agayn he wold gete me the same book for
> a copye.[4]

Caxton described the problems with his original text by blaming the
actions of previous scribes, instead of printers and compositors, but the
effects are largely the same: 'wryters haue abrydgyd it and many thynges
left out/ And in somme place haue sette certayn versys/ that he neuer
made ne sette in his booke'.[5] Notably, the young textual critic who offers
Caxton his father's 'very trewe' copy has no certain way of establishing
how closely it approximates Chaucer's own (if-ever-authorized) text: the
operation of the 'author function' in this late fifteenth-century example
depends as powerfully on the imagination of a correct authorial text as
does the twenty-first century assessment of textual inconsistency in *The
Lord of the Rings*.

Where the Gothic scribes of the fifteenth century and the other poets
discussed in the previous chapter saw the almost infinitely expandable
framework of the *Tales* as opportunity for their own continued play with
(and against) the 'moving target' original that structured the resulting
manuscripts, Caxton and his reader clearly understand the authorial
original to be a kind of fixed target, one which can and should be
approached by successive approximations. That such an authorial original lies in the realm of ideas, rather than in the nature of Chaucer's great
work, worries them not at all, and long before Tolkien's time it is clear it
had become part of even authors' thinking. Again, tracing the origin of
this change in perspective may prove impossible, and it is even likely that
Chaucer and his contemporaries anticipated it in some ways, but the
power of print to make the authorial original into an ideal construct of
great conceptual importance occurs with remarkable speed, and once
printing becomes widespread it quickly takes over as the dominant mode
of textual reproduction. If medieval writing was *variance*, in Cerquiglini's
terms, printed books find *variance* antithetical to what they mean, even
while they (often enough) depart from the physical exemplars they base
their reproductions upon. Likewise, printed books are not at all immune
to *variance*, even within a single printing (since corrections can be made

---

[4] W. J. B. Crotch, ed., *The Prologues and Epilogues of William Caxton*, EETS o.s. 176
(London: EETS, 1928), p. 91.
[5] Crotch, ed., *Prologues and Epilogues*, pp. 90–1.

in the forme for a page between the printing of one sheet and the next); but the ideology that shapes printed books now sees *variance* as a textual problem, a bug, rather than a feature.

Before leaving my unlikely comparison of *The Lord of the Rings* and *The Canterbury Tales*, it is perhaps useful to note how Tolkien also both echoes and reshapes the Gothicism of that other great Oxford writer of a British national mythology, Geoffrey of Monmouth. Like Monmouth, Tolkien presents *The Lord of the Rings* as a translation of an utterly inaccessible manuscript written in a doubly-inaccessible language. For Monmouth, as I argued in the last chapter, the *topoi* of the unique manuscript and of translation served to define his British source as a classic Gothic moving target, one that potential readers like William of Malmesbury and Henry of Huntingdon have no hope of finding. Tolkien, contrastingly, uses much of the space in his extensive Appendices precisely to present his work as a translation undertaken with the utmost care for accuracy; despite its fictionality, the original manuscript is presented as a fixed target that can be approached, even if only with difficulty and care. That is, Tolkien still invokes the inaccessible original, in ways quite superficially similar to Geoffrey of Monmouth, but Tolkien imagines the need to treat the inaccessible original as both authoritative and accurately reproduced in the act of translation.[6] To do so, of course, is merely to treat *The Lord of the Rings* as a book composed under the paradigm of print reproduction, where the entities reproduced are conceptualized as ideal and coherent and correct, and the goal of all reproduction is accuracy and precision, even though that goal can never be fulfilled. The accuracy claims in relation to Tolkien's supposed translation are close parallels to Tolkien's (and Anderson's) efforts to produce a printed edition with a truly correct and corrected text.

Editions

The edition, as I will argue here, is a specific sort of book, one rooted in the perception that an idealized version of a work is what the printed version of a work attempts to reproduce. That is, because editions are

---

[6] See Tolkien's Appendices throughout; for his discussion of translation in particular, see J. R. R. Tolkien, *The Lord of the Rings* (Boston: Houghton Mifflin, 2004), pp. 1133–8.

implicated in an economy of reproduction, they necessarily operate under the ideology of the logic of the copy; editions, however, attempt to ameliorate the failures inherent in the logic of the copy by asserting the opposite: editions are printed books that make explicit or implicit claims to the value and accuracy of the texts they transmit. Editions, of course, were indeed possible in previous eras: Jerome's fourth-century preparation of the vulgate Bible, for example, can rightly be deemed an edition, as it was both intended for reproduction and explicitly articulated its correctness as a remedy for the failures of reproduction. But when produced within the dominating paradigm of print reproduction, editions generally respond to their own inherent failure to be ideal by asserting their accuracy and authority.

A quick glance at Caxton's first printed version of *The Canterbury Tales* reveals the degree to which it is not, in fact, a fully articulated edition (STC 5082).[7] The poem begins, in this printed version, without preamble of any sort: after a three-line space for an initial letter 'w' to be added in by hand, the first printed characters make up the remainder of the first line of the *General Prologue*. There are no illustrations, no running headings, no printed marginal glosses: virtually none of the paratextual accompaniments used so well in the Ellesmere manuscript, and to a lesser degree in Hengwrt. Chaucer's own name is difficult indeed to find, until a reader encounters the verso of an unnumbered leaf more than half way through the book, where, after the interruption of the narrator's telling of *Sir Thopas*, the tale we now know as *Melibee* is prefaced by the brief, centred heading 'Sequitur Chawcers tale' which then begins at the top of the following page. The book as a whole ends with Chaucer's 'Retraction' and thus lacks any printer's mark, date, or colophon. The text printed, then, is limited to the very core of what we know as *The Canterbury Tales*, without most of the sorts of paratextual supports that can often be seen in manuscripts of the work, and it is difficult not to suspect that Caxton has largely stripped paratextual material in his copy manuscript from the printed version, in recognition that the 'text' of the

---

[7] My access to STC titles was through my library's access to the valuable *Early English Books Online* resource at <http://eebo.chadwyck.com/home>. My thinking about early printings of Chaucer has been shaped by my reading of Alexandra Gillespie, *Print Culture and the Medieval Author: Chaucer, Lydgate, and Their Books 1473–1557* (Oxford: Oxford University Press, 2006) and William Kuskin, *Symbolic Caxton: Literary Culture and Print Capitalism* (Notre Dame, IN: University of Notre Dame Press, 2008).

Tales does not include such things: glosses, running heads, marginal comments, and illustrations might well be supplied (along with numerous initial letters) by readers or professional rubricators, but for Caxton, they make no part of the ideal text he attempts to reproduce. This sifting of text from paratext already idealizes 'the text' as that which is worthy of reproduction, the first step in the direction of producing true editions. In this sense, even Caxton's first edition of the *Tales* does partake of the logic of the edition at a basic, fundamental level.

Of course, it is practically unimaginable that any early reader of Caxton's first printing of the *Tales* would have needed to wade through all those leaves of poetry to discover Chaucer's name: the purchaser of any such copy would surely have spoken with the seller, and the contents of the book would have been well known. My point is that the book, as it was reproduced, makes very little effort to do the work of identifying either the work or the author. To the degree that authorial names, titles, prefaces, and so on served conceptually in earlier periods to define, situate, and localize works intended for reproduction and distribution (a tradition often observed in the breach in Gothic literature's active play with authorship, titles, and moving target originals), Caxton's first printing of the *Tales* appears to indicate that print can dispense with explicit indicators of such things because print is (always already) reproduction. For Caxton to put the *Tales* into print was simultaneously to sift the grain of its text from its paratextual chaff and to obviate the need for the paratexts that once served to define the text in order to enable its reproduction.

And yet, within a mere handful of years, probably in 1483, Caxton was approached by the textual critic alluded to above and given the opportunity to reproduce a version of the *Tales* more in accord 'in many places vnto the book that Gefferey chaucer had made'.[8] The book still was printed without a title page, but now it opens with a two-page 'Prohemye' signed at the end by 'Wylliam Caxton' and clearly identifying 'Gefferey chaucer' as the 'first auctour and maker of thys book'.[9] Besides the various textual alterations involved, Caxton's second edition of the *Tales* now includes woodcut illustrations, and there are now running headings on each page, identifying the various tales and narrators. The likelihood that Chaucer's authorship

---

[8] Crotch, ed., *Prologues and Epilogues*, p. 91.
[9] Crotch, ed., *Prologues and Epilogues*, p. 91.

extends to the woodcut illustrations seems slim indeed, and the differing treatment of paratextual matters in the two printings reveals an important shift in Caxton's practice. Where the first printing of the *Tales* eliminated virtually all paratext as extraneous to the reproduction of the text, the failures of the first edition are remedied not only by printing a text held to be more correct, but also by redeploying various paratexts (implicitly or explicitly *not* authored by Chaucer) specifically to insist on accuracy and fidelity to Chaucer's own book. Such a strategy, of course, relies on readers' ability to distinguish between text and paratext, as the non-Chaucerian parts of the book now serve to authenticate the Chaucerian portions.

Nothing could, of course, be less Gothic. Whether deriving from Chaucer himself or from Adam Pinkhurst, the paratextual and textual divergences of the Ellesmere and Hengwrt manuscripts of the *Tales* each engaged in different ways with the Gothic 'moving target' nature of the original to produce different individual books in which the interaction between text and paratext was literally part of the game, because all manuscripts of the *Tales* were understood to differ on principle. The differences between manuscripts (or between one manuscript and Caxton's first printing) are the very problem that Caxton's second printing attempts to remedy: it is important to Caxton to announce that the remedy has been undertaken, and Caxton's 'Prohemye' locates the assertion of accuracy, authority, and authenticity in the paratext. The other newly included paratexts (running headings and woodcut illustrations), by differentiating themselves from Chaucer's text, thus exhibit Caxton's oversight of the text on every single page, serving both as guides for readers and as continuing promises or reminders of textual authority. Where the paratextual play of Chaucer's Gothic masterpiece (as embodied in the multiple prologues and narrators) encouraged additional layers of paratextual play in its manuscripts (glosses, illustrations, headings, additional tales), Caxton's two printings first eliminate paratexts almost entirely, then recontextualize them into assertions of editorial accuracy and control, precisely because they insist on a real difference between text and paratext. The paratextual game-pieces remain the same, but the rules of the game have changed.

To put the issue in slightly different terms, the 'moving target' nature of Gothic originals invited play between text and paratext as a typical and productive mode of *variance*, and in some works, authors themselves engaged in such play. In Caxton's world, however, the ideological contents of the very practice of print held that all copies of a printed book were notionally identical (however thoroughly such a notion failed in practice, due to variations in binding, rubrication, and even typographical changes). The ideology of print generated or depended upon the very conceptual possibility of an ideal, best text, a fixed target. The time involved in generating this non-Gothic perspective was very short indeed, as printed books were immediately possessed of a uniformity practically unimaginable in a manuscript culture, and that uniformity (operative even at the level of individual letter forms) denies the *variance* that defined Gothic reproduction.[10] One could (and still can) see right away that a printed book was not a manuscript, although it was reproducing one. The manuscript that the press reproduces, then, is conceptualized almost immediately as a fixed target, although one invisible to the readers of printed books. It is but a small step from there to the notion of an invisible best text, as even Caxton's 'Prohemye' to the second edition of the *Tales* suggests by its insistence on an association with Chaucer's own hand and manuscript, a copy 'that was very trewe/ and accordyng vnto hys owen first book by hym made'.[11] The visible printed text implies an underlying ideal text precisely because the printed text is so visibly not a manuscript.

The degree to which the notion that the printed book was understood as a reproduction of an ideal original might be confirmed, however, by a case in which the original was not nominally articulated as a manuscript at all. In Thomas More's 1516 *Utopia*, for example, the original that *Utopia* explicitly claims to reproduce is Hythloday's spoken narrative of Utopia, as received by More and Peter Giles, the addressee of an epistolary preface to Book 1.[12] In this letter, Giles is invited to correct More's text in order to ensure its faithfulness as a reproduction of Hythloday's speech; thus, Book 1 engages in one of the classic authenticating strategies of the edition.

---

[10] Although neither of Caxton's printings of *The Canterbury Tales* makes use of a title page, it is important to see that the separate title page takes off as an independent paratextual element in the years 1485–1500: see Margaret M. Smith, *The Title Page: Its Early Development, 1460–1510* (London and New Castle, DE: The British Library and Oak Knoll Press, 2000), fig. 3.2, p. 50. One suspects that the rise of the title page corresponds closely to the rise of the use of other paratexts under discussion here to help define the nature of the edition near the end of the incunable period.

[11] Crotch, ed., *Prologues and Epilogues*, p. 91.

[12] The letter to Giles is printed in Sir Thomas More, *Utopia: A New Translation*, Norton Critical Edition, trans. and ed. Robert M. Adams (New York: Norton, 1975), pp. 110–13. For the complex paratextuality of early editions of *Utopia*, see Terence Cave, ed., *Thomas More's Utopia in Early Modern Europe: Paratexts and Contexts* (Manchester: Manchester University Press, 2008), especially the useful Table I, p. 278.

Here, More's text does play with the troublesome boundary between text and paratext, as Book 1 has aspects of each, but More's play does not invoke a moving target original: Hythloday may be a dispenser of nonsense, as his name suggests to readers with sufficient Greek, but the fiction of *Utopia* presents his speech as the true original of the text being reproduced. Where Geoffrey of Monmouth and Marie de France and Chaucer utilized inaccessible originals to define their sources' moving target nature, More brings Peter Giles into the narrative precisely to counteract Hythloday's inaccessibility: Giles is the witness that swears to the accuracy of the repro-duction. That More is engaged in play is clear enough, but the joke plays out differently, in that Utopia (which, of course, is the very place that sup-posedly authorizes Hythloday's narrative) is not a hard-to-find or diffi-cult-to-access moving target, but an utterly absent one: NoPlace. For More, the joke ultimately lies in the status of his book as a simulacrum, a reproduced entity without an original at all. *Utopia*'s simulacral play with the machinery of the edition can be taken as another early statement on the very nature of the printed book as it operated on a different basis from the classic Gothic manuscript. The edition, in its fully formed exist-ence, always operates as a simulacrum, in that the original that is repro-duced is an ideal, in the realm of ideas rather than things: *Utopia*'s textual play centres precisely on identifying the simulacrum as essential to the nature of the edition.

A century and more after Caxton and More, the fundamental forms and effects of the edition had changed but little, as we might note from looking at the famous 'First Folio' of Shakespeare's plays from 1623.[13] Here, before the opening page of *The Tempest*, we find a series of para-textual materials at the opening of the book: verses 'To the Reader' by Ben Jonson; a title page, complete with an assertion of authenticity ('according to the True Originall Copies') and a large engraving of the author; an 'Epistle Dedicatorie'; a prose note to readers and more cele-bratory verses; a table of contents ('Catalogue') and ultimately a list of actors.[14] Where Caxton's 'Prohemye' identified his own earlier printing

---

[13] William Shakespeare, *Mr William Shakespeares Comedies, Histories, & Tragedies* (London: Isaac Iaggard and Ed. Blount, 1623) [STC 22273].

[14] Shakespeare, *Comedies, Histories, & Tragedies* (1623), fos. [i]v; [A1]r; A2r–v; A3r–[A8]r; note that the order of these pages differs in the West Virginia University Library copy from the typical order, with some pages having been being laid onto stronger sup-porting pages.

as flawed, Heminge and Condell as editors disparage previously available Shakespearean texts as 'diuerse stolne, and surreptitious copies,
maimed, and deformed by the frauds and stealthes of iniurious impos-
tors', which are now made available 'cur'd, and perfect of their limbes' as
if by some powerful *pharmakon* indeed.[15] To the degree that these paratexts identify the author, assert his importance, and argue for the original authority of the printed texts, they echo the effects of Caxton's
'Prohemye' to *The Canterbury Tales* quite closely. The inclusion of a table
of contents along with running headings and page numbers once again
demonstrates the publisher's or editors' attention to each page, despite
occasional (and well-known) slips: *Troilus and Cressida*, for example,
fails to appear on the table of contents, is presented among the histories,
and is largely unpaginated, leading scholars to conclude it was a late
addition. Likewise, in the Histories section, *2 Henry IV* begins on page 74,
and then the pagination of *Henry V* backs up to begin again at page 69;
this detail is somewhat surprisingly and confusingly indicated correctly
on the table of contents, which thus indicates the non-sequentiality of
the pagination in this section. But the way in which the 'True Originall
Copies' are invoked on the title page explicitly locates the source of the
Folio's authority in the copy-texts employed, which modern scholars
(through collation, in some cases) variously identify as manuscripts or
earlier printed quartos.

Remarkably, the Second Folio, which advertises itself on the title page
as a 'Second Impression' makes the same claim to authority based upon
the 'True Originall Copies'.[16] Yet it might be more accurate to suggest
that, in its practice, the Second Folio attempts to reproduce the First
Folio, as it was certainly a resetting, more than a true second impression.
Although Ben Jonson's 'To the Reader' and the title page are barely
changed, more dedicatory poems are now included, and the table of
contents now shows *Troilus and Cressida*, although dropping off all page
numbers. In the body of the book, *Troilus and Cressida* is now integrated
into the run of page numbers (1–30) among the tragedies, although
the anomalous page numbers for *Henry V* remain unchanged. Often, the
plays take exactly the same number of pages as in the First Folio, in the

[15] Shakespeare, *Comedies, Histories, & Tragedies* (1623), fo. A3r.
[16] William Shakespeare, *Mr William Shakespeares Comedies, Histories, & Tragedies*
(London: Robert Allot, 1632) [STC 22274].

Comedies and Histories often with the very same page numbers, suggesting the setting was accomplished in page-by-page fashion from the First Folio. But the claim to be based in 'True Originall Copies' as it stands in the Second Folio, then, is an inherited feature, rather than a new and competing claim to authenticity. The visual similarity of the Second Folio to the First does, however, make its own kind of claim of fidelity or accuracy, though connecting only the two printed versions to one another.

The 1664 'Third Folio', printed after the Restoration, might be expected to distinguish itself in various ways from the first two folios, and it is most famous, probably, for including *Pericles, Prince of Tyre*, as well as a variety of other plays now not generally felt to be Shakespearean.[17] The title page, interestingly, both announces the inclusion of these new texts and stakes the familiar claim that the book is 'The Third Impression' made 'according to the true Original Copies'. Again, many of the initial paratexts are, indeed, taken over from the earlier folios (although, again, clearly reset, rather than being a simple new impression), but now the pagination is continuous throughout the Comedies, Histories, and Tragedies, although *Pericles* re-initiates pagination at 1. The remaining new items then start yet again at page 1, although the remainder are numbered sequentially after *The London Prodigal* ends on page 16. The new items, as the title page makes clear, are included in an effort at completeness, and thus this edition explicitly attempts to remedy a perceived fault of the two earlier editions. The use of continuous pagination through the bulk of the book also seems likely to be an attempted remedy of a perceived fault. But note that the pagination used also sets off both *Pericles* and the other new additions as distinct, somehow, from the plays present in the first two folios.

Uniquely among the seventeenth-century Folios, the 1685 'Fourth Folio' of Shakespeare's works announces on the title page that it is the 'Fourth Edition' rather than merely a fourth impression, retrospectively identifying the earlier folios as editions in their own right, of course.[18]

[17] William Shakespeare, *Mr William Shakespear's Comedies, Histories, & Tragedies* (London: P. C., 1664) [Wing S2914]; the 1664 Third Folio was preceded by a 1663 printing without the seven newly included plays.

[18] William Shakespeare, *Mr William Shakespear's Comedies, Histories, & Tragedies* (London: H. Herringman, E. Brewster, and R. Bentley, 1985) [Wing S2915].

It regularizes some, but not all of the pagination idiosyncrasies of the Third Folio, beginning both the Comedies and the Histories at page 1, although including *Troilus and Cressida, Coriolanus, Titus Andronicus,* and *Romeo and Juliet* in numerical page-sequence with the Histories, before resetting yet again to 1 and then continuing sequentially to the end of the book, including the seven new items that first appeared in 1664. In returning to a pagination built around three sections each beginning at page 1, the Fourth Folio recaptures (but also reconfigures and partially regularizes) a feature of the pagination of the First and Second Folios. The initial paratexts remain textually similar to the earlier editions, although again they have been reset, often into a space-saving two-column format. Similarly, the list of original actors and the 'Catalogue' or table of contents now appear on a single page (Figure 5).

What the four seventeenth-century Shakespeare folios reveal, when considered together, is the extent to which the central characteristics of the edition were, in fact, operative, even in books that did not necessarily identify themselves as 'editions'. The edition is 'authorized' by the name of the original author, although that authority is generally articulated through the actions of editors, whose names either may appear (as in the case of Heminge and Condell) or may not appear (as no other editors' names appear in the later folios). The authority of the edition is often explicitly opposed to prior editions or versions, and generally editions use paratexts to make implicit or explicit claims of superiority (through accuracy, completeness, or other means) associated with the purposes of reproduction, often enough specifically commercial purposes (Heminge and Condell's note 'To the great Variety of Readers' addresses readers with the command, 'what euer you do, Buy'[19]). These are the basic tools and functions of printed editions.

In the later folios' insistence that they are reproducing the First Folio (by identifying themselves as 'Second Impression' and 'Third Impression' and insistently reprinting virtually identical prefatory materials), they manage, however, a remarkable kind of sleight-of-hand, substituting their admitted reproduction of a printed book for the First Folio's claim of reliance on 'True Originall Copies'—even as they often copy that very claim. As with the destruction of older exemplars of

---

[19] Shakespeare, *Comedies, Histories, & Tragedies* (1623), fo. A3r; this passage, of course, is reprinted in the later folios.

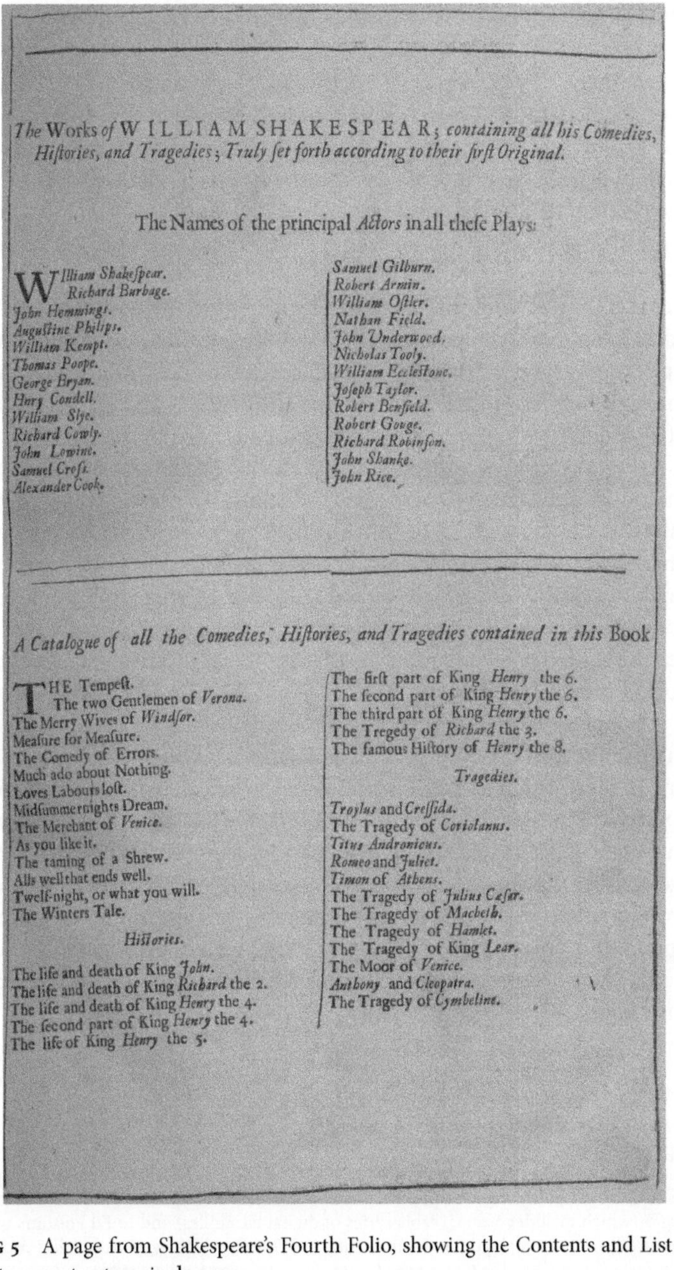

The Works *of* WILLIAM SHAKESPEAR; *containing all his Comedies, Hiſtories, and Tragedies; Truly ſet forth according to their firſt Original.*

The Names of the principal *Actors* in all theſe Plays:

William Shakeſpear.
Richard Burbage.
John Hemmings.
Auguſtine Philips.
William Kempt.
Thomas Poope.
George Bryan.
Henry Condell.
William Slye.
Richard Cowly.
John Lowine.
Samuel Croſs.
Alexander Cook.
Samuel Gilburn.
Robert Armin.
William Oſtler.
Nathan Field.
John Underwood.
Nicholas Tooly.
William Eccleſtone.
Joſeph Taylor.
Robert Benfield.
Robert Gouge.
Richard Robinſon.
John Shanke.
John Rice.

A Catalogue of all the Comedies, Hiſtories, and Tragedies contained in this Book

THE Tempeſt.
The two Gentlemen of *Verona.*
The Merry Wives of *Windſor.*
Meaſure for Meaſure.
The Comedy of Errors.
Much ado about Nothing.
Loves Labours loſt.
Midſummernights Dream.
The Merchant of *Venice.*
As you like it.
The taming of a Shrew.
Alls well that ends well.
Twelf-night, or what you will.
The Winters Tale.

Hiſtories.

The life and death of King *John.*
The life and death of King *Richard* the 2.
The life and death of King *Henry* the 4.
The ſecond part of King *Henry* the 4.
The life of King *Henry* the 5.
The firſt part of King *Henry* the 6.
The ſecond part of King *Henry* the 6.
The third part of King *Henry* the 6.
The Tregedy of *Richard* the 3.
The famous Hiſtory of *Henry* the 8.

Tragedies.

Troylus and *Creſſida.*
The Tragedy of *Coriolanus.*
Titus Andronicus.
Romeo and *Juliet.*
Timon of *Athens.*
The Tragedy of *Julius Cæſar.*
The Tragedy of *Macbeth.*
The Tragedy of *Hamlet.*
The Tragedy of King *Lear.*
The Moor of *Venice.*
Anthony and *Cleopatra.*
The Tragedy of *Cymbeline.*

FIG 5 A page from Shakespeare's Fourth Folio, showing the Contents and List of Actors reset onto a single page.

Image courtesy of the West Virginia and Regional History Collection, WVU Libraries.

Beowulf, the loss or destruction of the 'True Originall Copies' of Shakespeare's plays must almost certainly be understood in conjunction with the production of what does survive: the edition replaces the source materials because it reproduces not the originals themselves, but the ideal originals understood to lie behind them. In this sense, editions tend both to remediate manuscripts (in Bolter and Grusin's terms) and to at least attempt to render them invisible or unseeable.[20] It is part of the ideology of editions to claim or assert that the edited version is actually an improvement upon the manuscript, whether through multiplication alone, or through textual accuracy and authority, or even through simple typographic legibility. The printed edition may partake of a paradigm of reproduction defined by the logic of the copy, but the essential claim of all editions is that the machinery of the edition is intended or designed to overcome the failures of copying. So authoritative was the First Folio of Shakespeare that no readers needed to see Shakespeare's manuscripts for nearly a century, by which time the Folio's failures were clearly understood: but by that time the manuscripts had receded from sight entirely, and were lost. Rarely will we see the clash between reading and seeing reveal its effects so clearly, or so poignantly.

Examples of later authors who conceptualized their works through the paradigm of the edition are legion, and it is difficult to choose only one as representative. But it is useful, nevertheless, to compare the perspective of an inveterate reviser and tinkerer like Walt Whitman with that of the Gothic tinkerer Langland. Each seems to have taken his great work, *Piers Plowman* or *Leaves of Grass,* more or less literally as a life's work, written and revised almost continuously, some five hundred years apart; the 1891–2 edition of *Leaves of Grass* is widely known as the 'deathbed' edition, brought to press somewhat hurriedly during Whitman's final illness.[21]

---

[20] Jay David Bolter and Richard Grusin, *Remediation: Understanding New Media* (Cambridge, MA: MIT Press, 1999). In brief, Bolter and Grusin suggest that media 'remediate' when they promise a higher degree of faithfulness, accuracy, or immediateness than a prior medium.

[21] For my reading of Whitman's *Leaves of Grass* books in the next several paragraphs, I am indebted both to the online *Walt Whitman Archive* <http://www.whitmanarchive.org/> (which includes a remarkable series of digital facsimiles) and to Ed Folsom's wonderful illustrated 'catalogue and commentary', *Whitman Making Books, Books Making Whitman* (Iowa City: The Obermann Center for Advanced Studies, 2005).

Indeed, as the story of the 'deathbed' edition indicates, the interest Whitman took in *Leaves of Grass* as a printed book is notable, and the book's very title suggests both the proliferation of printed copies and the material form of a paper codex. A printer himself, Whitman set many of the pages of the self-published first edition into type, and he closely oversaw the typesetting of most of the American editions produced during his lifetime. Given what we know of Whitman's later practice of revision, it is impossible not to suspect that at least some of *Leaves of Grass* was composed or revised upon the composing stick itself: a born-printed text, existing for the very first time without any prior manuscript at all.[22] Born-printed, that is, if we understand the retrograde text upon the composing stick or in the printer's forme as something other than the text. Even here, then, the seemingly born-printed text exists explicitly as a reproduction (ink transferred to the page from the type itself); the sorting and redistribution of the type after printing, natural as it was, involved the destruction of Whitman's original handwork even more directly than in the case of many a manuscript.

Many Whitman manuscripts, of course, were saved: the nineteenth century saw a lively trade in many authors' original manuscripts, although whether their value as hedges against the failures of copying and printing outweighed their value as almost relic-like remains may not be fully determinable: to a degree, the two possibilities intertwine, and both were probably current, then as now. Yet it is probably important to note that Folsom describes, among the books catalogued at a 2005 Iowa exhibition, the posthumous 1902 Putnam edition of Whitman's *Complete Writings*, at least forty-two sets of which included manuscript material by the author.[23] Similar 'Manuscript Edition' sets were produced for a variety of authors, somewhat ironically associating the completeness claims of these editions with the literal fragmentation of at least some of the manuscript material that lay behind them, emphasizing or foregrounding the manuscript-as-relic dynamic, as well as emphasizing how printed editions obviated the textual value of the manuscripts that lay behind them.

[22] Folsom, *Whitman Making Books*, p. 4 suggests that 'Whitman probably never composed a line of poetry without, in his mind's eye, putting it on a composing stick', and at p. 32 Folsom writes 'He continued to look to the Romes' job shop as a place for quick typesetting to give him his poems in printed form,...do his final corrections on typeset copies,...and then turn in the Rome sheets to the publisher as printer's copy.'

[23] Folsom, *Whitman Making Books*, pp. 74–5.

It seems clear, then, that the relic-like status of authorial manuscripts—especially for authors in the print era—paradoxically emphasizes the way in which the print paradigm associates an almost immanent value to the 'original' text, a kind of acknowledgement that the reproduced text is flawed and thus devalued by comparison. A first edition of *Leaves of Grass*, of course, also now has a substantial monetary and textual value, and not only because Whitman set some of the type: but its value is partly analogous to the value of a manuscript because of the first edition's earliness, its rarity, and its closeness to the author's presumed first intentions. But such an observation serves to remind us of the degree to which editions often attempt to reproduce something that is essentially ideal, in the realm of ideas (an intention or a presumption), rather than a mere physical entity such as a manuscript.

Later editions of *Leaves of Grass*, especially those put out by commercial publishers, were generally set into type by other hands, but Whitman often still closely oversaw their setting. Surely we must therefore recognize Whitman's hand in the repeated decision *not* to use space on the title page to identify those later editions as 'new', or 'revised', or 'improved', or 'augmented' editions, just as Whitman's own name is generally absent from the title pages and (in the case of the first edition) absent from even the exterior of the book.[24] Such indicators of revised or improved editions, of course, serve the needs of publishers and marketing, and Whitman's habits of revising and augmenting thus take on an added significance given his apparent unwillingness to have later editions announce such additions and changes on their title pages. To the degree that later editions often had extensive tables of contents, new materials could be easily enough identified by those readers familiar with previous editions, but new readers, of course, might never have considered the textual history lying behind a particular edition of the book. As much as seems possible in the print era, Whitman allows various editions of *Leaves of Grass* to circulate freely and simultaneously, without necessarily requiring one edition to supplant or replace all

---

[24] Although a direct nod to Caxton's first edition of *The Canterbury Tales* seems unlikely, in the first edition, Whitman's own name first appears only in the middle of the first long poem, later titled 'Song of Myself': Folsom, *Whitman Making Books*, p. 11. One should note that while Whitman's name does not appear on the title page or exterior of the book, a striking engraved portrait of the author faces the title page as a frontispiece in the first edition.

others. But we must note both that this is a choice made (apparently by Whitman) and one that involves a kind of active working against the grain of the publishing practices of Whitman's time and place, even against the paradigm of print editions' conventional claims for authority-through-newness. Indeed, despite the general avoidance of labelling editions as second, third, and so on, Whitman himself did market an 'Author's Edition' of *Leaves* (1876), reminding us of print's seemingly inevitable connection to the realm of commerce. The history of Whitman's editions of *Leaves of Grass* shows both resistance to, and acceptance of, the commercial dimension of the edition's implicit and explicit claims to authority.

But as poets, the parallels between Whitman and Langland (whose great work was also constantly revised and edited, with various versions in circulation without paratextual indicators of sequence of composition or authorization) serve to remind us precisely that what was paradigmatically Gothic about the circulation and reproduction of Langland's poem is what runs counter to the practices of the print paradigm in relation to Whitman's book. Both poets do seem to have shared a habit of tinkering and revising, but those activities had different meanings, expressions, and implications in their different periods, deriving from the crucial differences between Gothic reproduction and print reproduction. Whitman, always at some level a printer himself, demonstrates an exceptional awareness of the nature and limitations of putting his book through various editions, even where (indeed, especially where) he attempts to undermine the logic of authority and value that editions and their paratexts most generally utilize.

What editions accomplish most effectively, of course, is to render texts legible. But as I suggested in the Introduction, legibility and visibility are opposed or in tension, and the very legibility of the edition both results in and is dependent upon the invisibility of the ideal text that the edition serves to reproduce. With surprising consistency, from Caxton's second printing of *The Canterbury Tales* to the present, printed editions not only remediate manuscripts (especially in their explicit or implicit insistence that their legibility or authority or correctness is superior to a manuscript), but also position the object of reproduction outside of books entirely, in the realm of language or ideas, where it can have a unique and coherent identity. Both operations, it is important to say, are necessary, but mutually contradictory: manuscripts are faulty, and in need of remediation, which indicates that the printed edition is superior, but at the same time, the printed edition, precisely by defining the original as ideal, becomes defined by its failures under the logic of the copy.

The facsimile

As a remedy for the failures of print reproduction, of course, the strategies employed by editions are decidedly Derridean *pharmakon*s, medicinal remedies that poison as they cure and that highlight the very gaps and *suppléments* that they claim to bridge. But over the years of the print era, a quite different strategy for remedying the failures of print has sometimes been used: the facsimile. Facsimiles take as their founding principle the idea that a manuscript (or other) 'original' text can be visually reproduced in order to grant readers the most direct sort of access to the ultimate source of textual authority. Of course, one might immediately point out that the mediation involved in facsimiles is itself a matter of representation, and that as a consequence, facsimiles, too, necessarily fail to deliver authenticity in any sort of direct fashion. But, as Siân Echard has effectively argued, 'the impulse to facsimile' has long been one of the main modes by which print reproduction has represented the past to readers and consumers.[25] To the degree to which the impulse to facsimile makes an explicit or implicit claim of immediacy, facsimiles also remediate both the sources they reproduce and the editions produced from those sources, in Bolter and Grusin's terms. As such, the impulse to facsimile really is inseparable, in some ways, from the impulse to produce editions, differing only in how the printed facsimile manages the work of remediation.

Indeed, the impulse to facsimile explicitly serves to encourage the act of seeing as an addition or adjunct to reading, rather than as an alternative to reading, because the motive for producing a facsimile is inseparable from the identification of a readable text. Because virtually all reproductive technologies prior to modern digitization were more expensive than the setting of type, facsimiles formerly tended to be produced only for texts with the highest degree of cultural or other value.

[25] Siân Echard, *Printing the Middle Ages* (Philadelphia: University of Pennsylvania Press, 2008).

Traced by Echard to the sixteenth-century printings of Anglo-Saxon texts and the 1610 printed image of the cross supposedly found on King Arthur's tomb at Glastonbury, facsimiles themselves, as Matthew Parker might have put it, began as kind of *Testimonie of Antiquitie* in relation to newly-printed works.[26] At its origins, then, the impulse to facsimile is a kind of hedge against the very possibility of the printed simulacrum, the printed work without any supporting authenticity: one cannot help but think of the sample Utopian alphabet printed in the 1516 first edition of More's *Utopia*, which indeed has remarkable affinities with the character tables used by Parker and other users of Saxon types discussed in Echard's first chapter.[27]

Notably, of course, early facsimiles are generally only partial, unless the text of interest is indeed very brief: usually, only a portion or sample of the text is presented in facsimile, with the rest translated into contemporary printed form, once the authenticating function of the facsimile has done its work. As such, these early facsimiles are adjuncts to the machinery of the printed edition, illustrative paratextual supports for the authority and accuracy of the printed books that contain them. The editions that these earliest printed facsimiles accompany remain the centre of readerly and visual interest.

In the nineteenth century, however, new technologies of reproduction are brought to bear, and facsimiles began to offer a variety of new possibilities. Two new modes of facsimile are especially important, I think. First, of course, is the full-fledged photographic or reproductive facsimile, which fulfils the promise of early facsimiles by extending to cover the full extent of the text in question: the 1882 publication of *Beowulf* in photographic facsimile was an early and important step in this particular direction.[28] But the second half of the nineteenth century also witnessed a remarkable vogue in the production of wax and plaster

[26] Parker, Archbishop of Canterbury from 1559 to 1575, seems to have been behind the publication of the earliest printed edition of an Old English text (an Ælfrician homily) in [Matthew Parker], *A Testimonie of Antiquitie* (London: John Day, 1566). Echard, *Printing*, p. 28 notes that Parker's use of an Old English type font conferred authority 'but not necessarily by the production of a true facsimile'.

[27] See Echard, *Printing*, pp. 25–31 for the use of Anglo-Saxon alphabets as early signs of authenticity; for the Utopian alphabet, see the facsimile page in More, *Utopia: A New Translation*, p. 116, and the discussion in Cave, ed., Utopia *in Early Modern Europe*, as well as the frontispiece to Cave's book, showing the Utopian alphabet from another early edition.

[28] Julius Zupitza, *Beowulf Reproduced in Facsimile*, EETS o.s. 77 (London: EETS, 1882).

casts of major sculptures; although such casts have often been devalued in the meantime and removed from university and museum collections, the Victoria and Albert Museum in London includes a pair of large interior courtyard spaces devoted to such casts (the Cast Courts), including casts of both Trajan's Column and the Ruthwell Cross. The textual component of these casts allows us a usefully revealing perspective on the nature and effect of facsimile technologies, especially in comparison to printed facsimiles, and it is to these cast technologies that I turn my attention first.

What the plaster casts of Trajan's Column and the Ruthwell Cross teach us most directly is how to assess just what it is that a facsimile reproduces. In the case of these physical sculptures, the reproduction very clearly intends to reproduce the thing itself: the column or cross-shaft as it exists *in situ* in Rome or in Ruthwell. The purpose of this type of reproduction is to allow the reproduced sculpture to stand at a different point in space, but to otherwise make visible to observers what is visible on the original (no attempt is made to actually reproduce the material of the originals, replacing stone with plaster). Such cast reproductions are inherently three-dimensional and full-sized; the technology of making casts gives them, in principle, a high degree of fidelity to the originals. But despite the technological investment in making such full-sized reproductions, the ideological content of these casts remains squarely focused upon their visibility: the cast of Trajan's Column at the V&A is cut into two sections, both to fit more easily into the interior space, and to allow somewhat better sightlines from both the main floor and an upper gallery. Likewise, the nature of such casts emphasizes the reproduction of the objects themselves at the expense of any surrounding or nearby context: in a sense, these monumental facsimiles, like Caxton's first printed edition of *The Canterbury Tales*, identify the object of interest as 'textual' in clear distinction to any surrounding context or paratextual material. The 1882 facsimile of *Beowulf* does much the same thing, reproducing the pages containing that poem, but not reproducing the pages containing the other poems or prose works in the manuscript.

To the degree that these reproductive casts serve to emphasize and delineate a split between text and context, then, it is important to recognize that even they partake of the essential nature of modern (print-like) reproduction. That is, where the moving target nature of Gothic originals led to an endemic boundary confusion (or play) between texts and paratexts, print-era reproduction takes the distinction between text and context as the very precondition for reproduction.[29] In that sense, these cast sculptures are themselves editions, in the sense addressed above: reproductions of a central 'text' (or 'text and object') with context or paratext stripped away, and with an essential implicit or explicit promise or assertion of accuracy, fidelity, and reliability. That so very many of these elements are left unexpressed and implicit in these sculptural reproductions only superficially differentiates them from printed editions of texts; in their ideological components, such reproductions seem to operate almost exactly like printed editions: these are print-era reproductions par excellence.

It is probably significant that the proliferation of full-fledged textual facsimiles (and the technologies for producing them) in the twentieth century was simultaneous with the decline in interest in cast sculpture collections: both trends probably result from the widespread influence of photography as a dominant method of visual reproduction. One might note, for example, that nineteenth-century lithographic facsimiles allowed for coloured reproductions long before colour photography; black-and-white photographs became the dominant mode of facsimile reproduction, however, because of their promise of scientific, rather than artistic, accuracy. Regardless, because the product of photography is usually a smallish two-dimensional image, both the three-dimensionality and the sheer size of reproductions like those in the V&A Cast Courts make them seem almost exotic today.

By contrast, the sort of manuscript facsimile we see in the 1882 facsimile of the *Beowulf* portion of London, British Library, Cotton Vitellius A. xv. seems anything but exotic today, a clear and direct ancestor of the contemporary proliferation of printed and digitized manuscript images. Then and now, the need or desire for a photographic facsimile exists clearly as a supplement to or corrective for the insufficiencies of printed editions of a work. Especially for a work surviving in a unique manuscript, the authority of the manuscript is of the highest level: even a flawed manuscript, understood as an imperfect copy of an even more

---

[29] This is not to say that print-era authors do not play with paratexts: of course they do, as both More's letter to Giles and Tolkien's extensive Appendices remind us, to consider only examples already discussed. But print-era authors' play is a kind of play *against* the constraints of the medium of print, while Gothic play with paratexts is play *within* the outlines of Gothic reproduction.

authoritative original, may still stand as the best testimony to that original version. What a photographic facsimile offers to readers, then, is the promise of bypassing the mediation of editorial intervention: the facsimile literally remediates the edition, promising to offer better, clearer access to what it reproduces than an edition possibly can. That is, where an edition insists that the original is invisible (because ideal), the facsimile appears to promise the visibility of authenticity itself. In short, where editions derive or generate authenticity through the actions of editors, printers, and publishers, facsimiles assert that at least some sorts of authenticity are visible, and thus subject to visible reproduction.

Even so, it is important to state clearly that printed editions attempt to reproduce an ideal original, one that is true and correct in a fashion that is sure to be undermined by any actual, physical representation, while facsimiles simply promise to reproduce an older reproduction of the same original. The case of the facsimile of the *Beowulf* manuscript is therefore especially revealing, as the *Beowulf* manuscript, as I argued in my first chapter, was very probably not conceptualized as a reproduction of anything, until modern readers made it into one by the very act of constructing both an edition and the ideal original that the edition necessitates. The facsimiles of the Hengrwt and Ellesmere manuscripts of *The Canterbury Tales* are likewise predicated on modern readers' understanding or belief that these particular manuscripts have an especially close relationship to Chaucer's controlling original: a belief almost certainly at odds with Chaucer's (and Adam Pinkhurst's) probable understanding of all manuscripts of the *Tales* as copies of a moving target original, an original that was necessarily (and usefully) lacking a coherent authorial form.[30] That is, while the publication of facsimiles serves, at one level, to attempt to remediate editions (by improving readers' access to the locus of authority that underwrites editions), these medieval examples make it clear that facsimiles are themselves also a symptom of a central belief about texts and textuality that also underwrites editions. Facsimiles exist because print editions necessarily fail as reproductions (through the ideology that all print reproductions are

---

[30] One should note, of course, the logic that makes facsimiles from Hengwrt and Ellesmere because they are close to Chaucer is the same as the logic of Caxton's early reader, who offers Caxton a copy-text that is also held to be close to Chaucer, as noted at the beginning of the chapter.

understood as failures), and the makers of facsimiles attempt to reproduce the physical manuscript as the locus of authority and authenticity, rather than the ideal version of the text.

Because the purpose of facsimiles is to make visible a version of the text asserted to have authority or authenticity, facsimiles appear to remedy the failures of editions, by refocusing readers' attention upon a visible, rather than ideal, text. In this sense, one might assume that facsimiles contrast visibility with legibility in a useful new way, distinct from the operation of editions. And yet, facsimiles' necessary participation in the ideology of print-era (and now, digital) reproduction itself marks the degree to which they participate in the same ideology of print-era reproduction that enables editions. To put it in other terms, when we say facsimiles remediate editions, we merely say (along with Bolter and Grusin) that facsimiles, like typographical printed books, are media: what is important here is that the mode of mediation embodied by a facsimile is foreign to both non-media books (like the *Beowulf* manuscript) and to moving target media like Chaucerian manuscripts.

The failures of facsimiles of Anglo-Saxon and Gothic manuscripts reveal themselves in the ways that these types of manuscripts themselves refuse the notion of an ideal, controlling original, but of course even early printed books have become subject to the impulse to facsimile. Perhaps no facsimile of an early printed book is more revealing than Charlton Hinman's facsimile of Shakespeare's First Folio, which is, as Hinman notes, not a facsimile of any particular book, but rather an attempt to represent 'an ideal copy of the First Folio of Shakespeare: one in which every page is not only clear and readable throughout but represents the latest or most fully corrected state of the text'.[31] As Hinman notes further, 'such an ideal representation of the Folio is not now, and almost certainly never has been, realized in any actual copy of the edition'.[32] It is, in short, nothing less than a facsimile edition: an attempted reconstruction of the 'ideal' form of the First Folio, the principles of textual criticism applied not to the linguistic contents of the works, but rather to the pages (and photographs of pages) that are the basis of reproduction. What such an example reveals with startling clarity is the degree

[31] Charlton Hinman, ed., *The First Folio of Shakespeare: The Norton Facsimile* (New York: W. W. Norton, 1968), p. xxii.

[32] Hinman, ed., *First Folio*, pp. xxii–xxiii.

to which the imagination of an ideal version of a book nevertheless always still underwrites printed facsimiles: although Hinman's access to the Folger Library's extensive collection of First Folios gave him unprecedented access to a range of pages and photographs to choose among, all printed (and now digital) facsimiles actively or passively select photographs that make most clearly visible what the editors of the facsimiles believe ought to be visible to a careful reader of the manuscript or book. Indeed, sometimes facsimiles go even further: the 1882 facsimile of *Beowulf* went into a second edition, in 1959, with new photographs, including a number taken under ultraviolet light, literally making visible what the human eye cannot see under normal lighting conditions.[33]

All of this discussion is merely to say, of course, that printed facsimiles remain printed books. To a degree, they do attempt to remedy the failures of printed editions by making visible a state of the text which is associated with a high degree of textual authority or authenticity: the implicit claim is that the mediation undertaken by editions can be undone, to a degree, by recourse to the facsimile, which therefore remediates the edition. But printed facsimiles always are themselves editions, still reliant on presenting an ideal form of whatever it is that they reproduce, and by insisting, via a variety of paratextual forms, on the accuracy, fidelity, and trustworthiness of what they show, even if what they show in their reproductions is now a representation of a physical entity, rather than a representation of an ideal one. Although the technology employed in the photographic edition is distinct indeed from the hand-set type of Gutenberg and Caxton, the ideological underpinnings of modern photographic facsimiles appear to be inseparable from the textual ideology of print more generally, in which editions operate to make readable a text that is, ultimately, ideal, both leading to and springing from the inherent failure, at one level or another, of all attempts to represent it.

Because facsimiles promise to make a physical text visible, rather than an ideal text, they may well seem to reconfigure the relationship between seeing and reading, between visibility and legibility. But whether we consider Hinman's facsimile edition of the First Folio, or the ultraviolet photographs of Cotton Vitellius A. xv., or many another example, it is

---

[33] Julius Zupitza, *Beowulf Reproduced in Facsimile*, 2nd edition, with an Introductory Note by Norman Davis, EETS o.s. 245 (London: Oxford University Press, 1959).

probably important to acknowledge that all facsimiles are intended to work in conjunction with more traditional editions, rather than to actually supplant them. One uses the facsimile to understand the text, not to be the text or even to represent the text. One does not read a facsimile, then, one consults it. The facsimile, under the print paradigm, is understood to be a reproduction of a particularly authentic or authoritative representation of the text—which itself still lies somewhere else, at another remove. What facsimiles make visible is indeed important, but it is important within the paradigm of print-era reproduction, rather than outside of it.

Conclusions

Printed books, whether set from movable type or not, facsimile or otherwise, appear to be governed by an ideological reliance that identifies the legible, non-paratextual content of a book as a reproduction of an invisible, ideal original, and this conception becomes so dominant during the print era that it comes to be understood as a defining feature of textuality itself. To take just a single example, the differences between a photographic facsimile of the Hengwrt manuscript of *The Canterbury Tales* and a more traditionally printed edition of *The Tales* are very real, and very important, but to the degree that both understand their investment in reproduction as invested in accuracy and fidelity to an ideal original, both are characteristic of the print era, and both are essentially foreign to the nature of Chaucer's great work. Until all surviving manuscripts of *The Canterbury Tales* are available in facsimile, and until none of them is understood by readers to have a higher degree of authenticity or authority, we shall inhabit a textual culture that redefines works according to its own version of textuality as a matter of course.

And that is, of course, as it should be: all readers must make and remake texts as part of the very process of making meaning. And yet a conscious attention to our acts of remaking is also important, as well as attention to how our own version of textuality affects our understanding of what we read.

From another perspective, what print (as a practice, a phenomenon, a technology, and an ideology) accomplishes is to insist that the ideological uniformity of the output of the press corresponds to an ideal, pure, correct original form of the text. Whether that original is considered as authoritative due to closeness to an authorial version, or to explicit authorial authorization, or to coherence to an ideal form of presentation, or to correctness according to culturally specific standards and practices, or even to other processes and ideas, print as we know it in our tradition naturalizes the very notion of an ideal form for a text. But such naturalization, of course, emphasizes the ideological nature of the interlinking of these concepts. The reality, of course, is that print reproduction remains equally subject to the logic of the copy: printed texts always fail at representing the ideal form of texts precisely because printed copies are real, rather than ideal.

The importance of such a concept of textuality can hardly be overstated, and it seems clear that theorists of writing and literary production, and perhaps even of language, have often enough taken this position as definitive of the textual condition itself. What I hope to have accomplished in this chapter (and in this book) is to have shown how this concept is especially closely linked to the practices and concerns of print itself, and that it expresses itself in a particular kind of book that we can usefully label 'the edition'. The reasons for doing so are twofold: first, doing so has the effect of defining and historicizing the edition as a particular variety of textual structure, whether produced under the paradigm of print or not. An edition, as I have described it here, is any text that defines itself through its own self-insistence on its adherence as a text to an ideal original, whether what we are considering is a scholarly edition, a first edition, or even a pirated or abridged edition. Editions define one component of their textual contents as a 'text' which is more or less explicitly distinct from its surrounding paratexts. The distinction between text and paratext is thus essential to the nature of an edition; further, the central purpose of the paratext in an edition is always to assert or articulate the value of the printed 'text' via its association to the ideal form of the text.

Besides historicizing and defining the edition as a particular sort of text (one that itself separately defines a subset of its own contents as the 'true' text), the value of my association between editions and the ideology of print serves to encourage readers to resist the habit of seeing every text (especially those from manuscript periods) through the lens of editions: the paratexts surrounding Anglo-Saxon or Chaucerian works may be similar in form, and even content, to the paratexts employed in editions, but they operate differently in context. In short, our habit of reading virtually all literary texts in modern editions needs to be recognized and understood as our own habitual, and possibly even necessary, mode of making and remaking them to suit our own textual needs. To the degree that we are committed to a historicist understanding of works, however, sometimes we may need to put aside both the machinery and the ideology of the edition.

Interlude 3

Print to Comics

The first edition of Thomas Pynchon's *V.*, published by J. B. Lippincott in 1963, has a handful of unusual typographical features, the most striking of which is the copyright page (Figure 6).[1] The contents of this page are quite typical: copyright notice, permission statement, notices of the physical book's manufacturer and designer. The layout, however, is unusual: all the material on the copyright page is laid out in the shape of a downward-pointing triangle, closely nestled within the large capital 'V' of the book's title (which is printed on the recto side of the same leaf). The 'V' of the title can easily be seen through the paper in the first edition copies I have handled, and the positioning of the copyright material seems anything but coincidental.

It is important, I think, to recognize the degree to which this bit of typographic display accomplishes two things simultaneously. First, it takes a bit of linear language and structures it as a two-dimensional unit. Second, it shapes a bit of material usually considered to be paratextual into a form that helps articulate the meaning of the novel itself. To the degree that this paratextual copyright page material is thus pulled into the text of the novel, it engages in a breaking down of the text/paratext split that has been as productive for literary authors in the print era as it was for Chaucer and Marie de France, although configured somewhat differently. But in the way in which it accomplishes this end by employing

---

[1] Thomas Pynchon, *V.* (Philadelphia: Lippincott, 1963), p. [4].

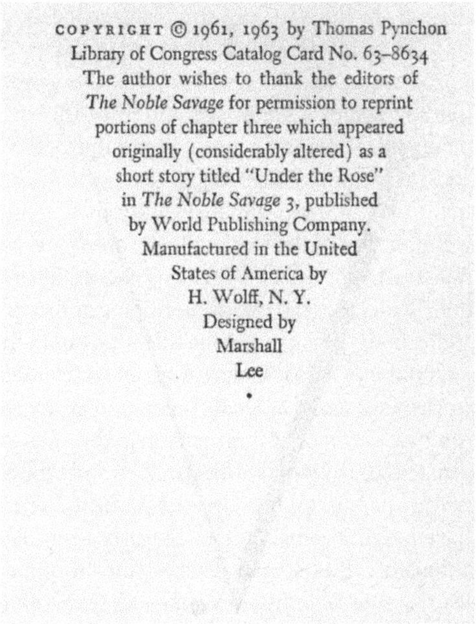

COPYRIGHT © 1961, 1963 by Thomas Pynchon
Library of Congress Catalog Card No. 63–8634
The author wishes to thank the editors of
The Noble Savage for permission to reprint
portions of chapter three which appeared
originally (considerably altered) as a
short story titled "Under the Rose"
in *The Noble Savage* 3, published
by World Publishing Company.
Manufactured in the United
States of America by
H. Wolff, N. Y.
Designed by
Marshall
Lee
•

FIG 6 The copyright page [from first edition] from *V.: A Novel* by Thomas Pynchon. Copyright © 1961, 1963 by Thomas Pynchon. Reprinted by permission of HarperCollins Publishers.

typography two-dimensionally, *V.* reminds readers that, at least sometimes, a printed text cannot be understood as representing only a work in language. Two-dimensional texts are visible, and they articulate some of their meaning by means that cannot be reduced to the linearity of continuous language.

And thus, there is one additional point about facsimiles that I think it is important to make: facsimiles, too, always bring multidimensionality to a printed literary work. That is, traditional, typographical printing works hand-in-hand with Tanselle's conception of literature as art executed in the medium of language because the relentless linearity of type (one letter after another, sequenced in space from beginning to end) matches the relentless linearity of language (a continuous stream of sounds and pauses, flowing unidirectionally through time). Indeed, it seems likely to me that Tanselle's conception of the nature of literature has been shaped by the linearity of print (and by the way print articulates an ideal original) in ways that he does not fully acknowledge. Printed facsimiles, by contrast, make the unit of reproduction not the letter or even the word, but the two-dimensional photograph or other image, and three-dimensional facsimiles of monuments like Trajan's Column or the Ruthwell Cross take the entire object itself as the unit of reproduction.

In emphasizing two- or three-dimensionality, then, facsimiles do open the door for a conception of the work of literature, or even the book, as a non-linear, non-linguistic entity. Hinman's facsimile of Shakespeare's First Folio, after all, includes the two-dimensional author portrait, as well as the visually effective type-layout of the title page (and other pages). But as even such a familiar example makes clear, all textual illustrations, and all typographic displays, stand as challenges to our conception of the text as linear: it is only an aspect of our immersion in the ideology of print-era reproduction that tends to associate illustrations and typographic display on title pages with paratext. Of course, there have been many writers indeed who have fought against literary linearity, on title pages, in their use of illustrations or other spatial devices, and in other ways as well: besides Sterne's *Tristram Shandy* and Vonnegut's *Breakfast of Champions*, one thinks immediately of George Herbert's 'The Altar', or Mallarmé's *Un Coup de Des*, or e. e. cummings's 'r-p-o-p-h-e-s-s-a-g-r'. Even Blake's watercolours, to say nothing of the examples of retrograde writing discussed in the Introduction, above, make the two-dimensional size and shape of the writing support or printed surface itself a part of the literary effect of the work. These works all insist upon two-dimensional meanings in addition to the linearity of what can be read aloud, since reading aloud itself insists upon linearity. To the degree that reading aloud remains possible in relation to a work of literature, that work emphasizes reading at the expense of seeing, and editions can change page layout, typeface, and other visual features with relative impunity. But where reading aloud is most directly challenged, the work of literature attempts to move out of the realm of linearity, and hence into the realm of seeing as well as reading. But it follows that one thing that authors who utilize two- or three-dimensionality are accomplishing is to challenge fairly directly the ideological understanding of the printed book as a container for (or representation of) a linguistic work.

The greatest proliferation of multidimensional literature, however, is surely the genre of comics, which got its start as a coherent tradition largely in the nineteenth century but with a remarkable blossoming in the twentieth. Where the digital revolution, with its ability to translate everything into a sequence of digital bits, captures and even extends the ideologically relentless linearity of print, the genre of comics takes its very form as a critique of typographical print reproduction, both insisting upon a two-dimensional presentation and generally eschewing typography and insisting upon the visibility of the author's or artist's handwork. It is to comics that I turn in my final chapter.

| 4 |

Comics Textual Production

The 'Foreword' to the 2011 volume of the *Best American Comics* series opens with the following remarkable claims from Jessica Abel and Matt Madden, the co-editors of the series:

> Comics is a printed medium. And now it's also a digital medium. What it isn't is a *direct* medium, like drawing or painting: there is no 'original' comic to read. The pages that have the ink on them may be beautiful to look at and they may offer loads of information for fans and researchers, but most people will agree that it's not really a comic until it has been reproduced.[1]

If taken at face value (which is, of course, exactly what I wish to do), the central claim here is simply that comics have a radically different relationship to the technology of printing than conventionally (typographically) printed texts do. In the terms of my discussion from the last chapter, comics are neither editions (engaged in representing an original that lies elsewhere) nor facsimiles (engaged in visually representing an authoritative state of a text): comics are a new and different *kind* of text. The importance of comics lies not only in the ability of comics works to incorporate images and text in two-dimensional or three-dimensional

---

[1] Jessica Abel and Matt Madden, 'Foreword', in Alison Bechdel, ed., *The Best American Comics 2011* (Boston: Houghton Mifflin, 2011), p. vii.

structures of meaning, but also in their new configuration of the very practices, principles, and ideologies of texts, technologies, and reproduction.

What I hope to accomplish in this chapter is to suggest the degree to which Abel and Madden's remarkable claims are, in fact, essentially correct, developing more or less straightforwardly from, on one hand, the histories of textual and reproductive practices outlined in my first three chapters. On the other hand, of course, comics also differ from that history through their incorporation of a visual or visible component that cannot be reduced to language alone: comics necessarily extend beyond the typographic. At the same time, I examine the contemporary practice of comics as exemplified primarily in the works of Chris Ware and Art Spiegelman, as a first step in working out the implications and significance of comics' unique and innovative configuration as a reproductive textual practice. The comics book is a new kind of book, and the comics text is a new kind of text, and even now the critical understanding of comics remains in its infancy. But turning our attention to this new sort of text is of the utmost importance for understanding contemporary textuality, including in the digital realm.

Defining comics

Although most of us probably feel like we can recognize a work of comics when we encounter one, it is nonetheless useful to step back for a moment and address just how we define comics as a medium, and why it is appropriate to treat comics as a species of text in the first place. Scott McCloud, comics creator and theorist, has developed what is probably the most widely accepted definition of comics, though it has received various criticisms, and probably needs modifying or updating. In McCloud's succinct formulation, comics involve 'Juxtaposed pictorial and other images in deliberate sequence, intended to convey information and/or to produce an aesthetic response in the viewer'.[2] Obviously, this definition relies upon a conception of authorial intention, and its

---

[2] Scott McCloud, *Understanding Comics: The Invisible Art* (New York: HarperPerennial, 1994), p. 9.

exclusion of one-panel comics is a well-known weakness.[3] Further, while McCloud seems to contemplate only two-dimensional images being juxtaposed, his definition does open the door for juxtapositions or sequences of three-dimensional sculptures to be read as comics.

McCloud's definition, however, allows him to include a vast array of historical examples beneath its umbrella, including Egyptian wall paint- ings, Mayan painted codices, and the Bayeux Tapestry. The cost of including such items, it must be pointed out, is that comics, for McCloud, essentially functions as a mode of reading juxtaposed images that oper- ates outside of and beyond specific historical and historicizable tradi- tions, even though most of the rest of his book involves only an extended discussion of the workings of the twentieth-century Western comics tra- dition. Abel and Madden's insistence that comics must be reproduced to be comics, of course, works quite precisely to exclude paintings and tap- estries (even juxtaposed ones): Hogarth's *Rake's Progress* paintings are not comics, according to such a claim, but the printed engravings derived from them are. And it seems to me that this sort of modification is indeed needed for McCloud's definition: just as print is a medium for which reproduction is necessary, comics is as well.[4] Indeed, to the degree to which comics reproduction operates as a response to or comment upon the workings of print reproduction, comics originate in the realm of print, and their migration to digital domains occurs as a separate issue to be addressed and understood, just as the migration of printed texts to digital form involves an important change. Digital texts are not printed, and digital comics are equally distinct from printed ones, although reproduction applies to both.

Ultimately, I believe that the medium of comics gets its impetus (in both a historical and an ideological sense) as a response to the workings of print reproduction precisely through the visible foregrounding of the author's hand (and handiwork) as opposed to the anonymity and uniformity of typography. And despite some early experiments, until

---

[3] One significant critique of McCloud's definition that attempts to rescue the single- panel cartoon is Robert C. Harvey, 'Comedy at the Juncture of Word and Image', in Robin Varnum and Christina T. Gibbons, eds., *The Language of Comics: Word and Image* (Jackson: University Press of Mississippi, 2001), pp. 75–96.

[4] The case of a book produced on a printing press in an edition of one is the limiting case, of course. My formulation here treats such an item as an object of art, not as a printed book.

digital technology brought its transformations, virtually all of the written language in comics was hand-lettered, rather than set in type; of course, computers now allow written language to be inserted into images that is neither hand-lettered nor truly typographic.[5] What print-style comics reproduction makes visible is always the product of an author's hand, a kind of manuscript, and this aspect of comics is just as important as the two-dimensional import of the 'images' component of McCloud's definition is important in responding to the implicit linearity of print. To the degree that comics does respond to the reproductive ideology of print, however, comics offers to teach us a great deal, both about print and about alternatives to print.

If we can modify McCloud's definition, then, comics (as I will discuss the form in this chapter) is a textual medium defined by the technology of print reproduction, in which juxtaposed pictorial images (or a 'single-panel' juxtaposition of word and image) function together for aesthetic or other purposes. Internet comics, of course, are excluded by this specific definition, although modifying my definition to read 'defined by the technology of print or digital reproduction' might serve if we found it necessary to include them. Yet it remains my conviction that the nature of digital reproduction is sufficiently different from print reproduction to suggest that the visual similarity of comics reproduced in the two different modes obscures a more fundamental difference.

Central to my definition, of course, is the claim that comics is a textual medium; efforts to define comics as a kind of hybrid of textual and visual forms misrepresent the essentially textual nature of the comics work. And it is important to note that the textual nature of comics extends even to wordless or 'silent' comics, which operate almost wholly as sequenced, reproduced images. But the acts of interpretation that make meaning from juxtaposed or sequenced images (or from the juxtaposition of one image and an associated script) are acts of reading, and not only in the common habit of referring to the act of 'reading comics' as opposed to looking at them. McCloud's definition insists that juxtaposed images be in 'deliberate sequence', and while I would put the burden on

---

[5] Likewise, online webcomics sometimes dispense with the author's hand for both images and text, making use of pre-existing clip-art, for example, or reusing the very same artwork for each installment of a long-running series. Again, computer mediation changes the nature of the mode of reproduction.

the reader, rather than on the deliberateness of the comics creators, it is the act of interpretive reading or meaning-making that underlies both positions. Comics works are printed works, read interpretively even in the absence of an explicit linguistic component: they might be best understood as texts that must incorporate a non-linguistic component.

Certainly, in the general case, comics works seem to meet the two complementary definitions of 'text' that I hypothesized in the Introduction, above. Comics texts, according to my definition (and according to the logic of Abel and Madden) are always implicated in an economy of reproduction. Likewise, they are generally accompanied or characterized by a suite of paratextual features that serve to define their boundaries: comics works generally come with an author's name attached (and often enough an artist's name as well, and both can function in the role of author); a title; and well-defined boundaries.[6] A fine (and fairly early) literary example might be Milt Gross's wonderful 1930 (almost) wordless comics novel, *He Done Her Wrong*, which features a hand-drawn title page (giving title, subtitle, author's name, and publication information) as well as a typeset dedication page and authorial foreword.[7] That these features are understood to be paratextual, not textual, might be confirmed by looking at the 2005 Fantagraphics 'redesigned edition' of *He Done Her Wrong*, which alters both the title of the book itself and the title page, as well as eliminating the dedication page and authorial foreword entirely.[8] The Fantagraphics editors' removal or alteration of these elements in their own reproduction of the text (even as it remains almost entirely wordless) confirms a perception of their function as essentially paratextual. Indeed, even the subtitle of the 1930 printing ('*and Not a Word In It*') suggests that we should locate the words of the dedication

---

[6] For the comics artist configured in the author position, see Thomas A. Bredehoft, 'Style, Voice, and Authorship in Harvey Pekar's (Auto)(Bio)Graphical Comics', *College Literature* 38.3 (2011), 97–110.

[7] Milt Gross, *He Done Her Wrong: The Great American Novel and Not a Word In It—No Music, Too* (Garden City, NY: Doubleday, Doran & Company, 1930). The foreword, notably, is printed on the verso of the dedication page, facing the first image of the novel proper; the pages throughout are unnumbered.

[8] Milt Gross, *He Done Her Wrong: The Great American Novel* (Seattle: Fantagraphics, 2005), copyright page (unnumbered); this edition's pages are also completely unnumbered. On the front wrap (although not on the title page), the title of the book is given as *He Done Her Wrong: The Great American Novel (With No Words)*.

and foreword (and the title, author's name, and title page as well) in the realm of paratext.[9]

Comics, then, must be something quite remarkable: a species of text, according to the definitions I have been using throughout, but a kind of text that must always include a non-linguistic component, and which can, indeed, even dispense with linguistic material entirely. It is important to say clearly, however, how a work of comics differs indeed from a book of pictures, such as a scrapbook or album, even if printed and reproduced. These other entities can always be distinguished from comics by the circumstance that comics works demand an act of interpretive reading across the boundary between juxtaposed elements. An album or scrapbook is always defined by a principle of accumulation or aggregation; a work of comics is defined by the logic of juxtaposition. Likewise, although many illustrated books also feature juxtapositions of words and images, illustrated literary books generally make use of images primarily as paratexts, not as a central part of the text itself. To the degree that visual elements do sometimes begin to play a role in the meaning-making strategies of the text, some literary texts (one thinks again of Vonnegut's drawings in *Breakfast of Champions*) do indeed partake of the comics-like power of juxtaposition. But in non-literary genres, of course, diagrams, illustrations, and plans have long served as central parts of texts, rather than as mere paratexts. What an understanding of the comics mode of textual meaning does is to focus our attention on the question of whether an image functions textually or paratextually, whether the book in question is literary or not. Printed textual images can rightly be considered as comics, or at least as partaking of the nature of comics; printed images serving as paratexts cannot. What comics as a literary genre accomplishes is to bring to the world of literary expression a mode of juxtapositional meaning-making that has long been operative in non-fictional genres that make use of images that go beyond mere illustration.

All of this discussion, however, reveals that the two necessary elements in any definition of comics textuality must be juxtaposition and reproduction. It is from this definitional position that I proceed throughout the remainder of this chapter.

---

[9] Below, I will suggest in my discussion of Spiegelman's *Maus* books that such a view of a real text/paratext split in comics works like *He Done Her Wrong* may be illusory, and an artefact of a viewpoint that sees comics as analogous to printed, typographic works.

Comics works are not facsimiles

As noted above, Abel and Madden's insistence that 'it's not really a comic until it has been reproduced' is inescapably linked to their claim that 'there is no "original" comic to read'.[10] In the terms I have used throughout the present book, the suggestion is clear that comics do not function like facsimiles, attempting to visually reproduce a highly authoritative state of a text. At first glance, the claim appears to be obviously untrue: as a rule, comics are indeed drawn by hand, and the signs of that handdrawing are exactly what get reproduced (non-typographically), just as facsimiles of manuscripts make the handwork of authors or scribes visible. But a second glance reveals that the ideological grounding of the facsimile differs from the ideological grounding of the reproduced work of comics, and the claim that comics are not facsimiles is both surprising in its implications and compelling.

At the most superficial level, the widespread use of colour in many of the most familiar comics forms (e.g., Sunday comics pages, or superhero and 'funny animal' and virtually all traditional comic books) illuminates the key issue: in almost every case, the original artwork for a comics work is done in black ink on a white surface, and the author's or artist's hand leaves the work in black and white. Colour, when it is added, is added during the process of reproduction, rather than during what might be supposed to be the production of the 'original.' In a very basic sense, then, what is reproduced in the case of colour comics is, indeed, not what appears visibly in the author's or artist's original: the drawing is not the original of the reproduction, in that the reproduction differs from the original in a crucial, central way. Although it may not be as obvious, the same is clearly true for black and white comics as well.

All comics creators, it is important to recognize, draw what they draw with the active intention that it be reproduced: their handwork is, in purpose and effect, a preliminary stage in the production of the comics work, which does not occur until the process of printed reproduction is complete. And not only is original comics art often coloured during the production process, but it also is generally greatly reduced in size; in the typical case, the artwork is intentionally distinct from the comics work

---

[10] Abel and Madden, 'Foreword', p. vii.

itself because of their essential differences in size. For these reasons, the production of a comics work and its reproduction are ultimately indistinguishable, even while the making of the original artwork remains an important stage of pre-production. Although comics works depend upon reproduction as part of their very nature, the ideological relationship of comics to the process of reproduction is different from non-comics printed texts, and from facsimiles in particular. Facsimiles, as discussed in Chapter 3 above, attempt to make authority or authenticity itself visible in some fashion; to the degree that facsimiles remediate editions, they are explicitly dependent upon the idea, if not the reality, of existing editions. Comics works, by contrast, do not depend on editions in any way at all, and they certainly do not remediate them: the 1930 printing of Gross's *He Done Her Wrong* does not remediate any other printed text, as it is, indeed, its own first appearance in the world. The effect of defining the comics work as something necessarily reproduced means that the comics text also does not remediate the original artwork—because in the context of a comics work the supposed 'original' is, in fact, not truly original, but merely preliminary.

As Abel and Madden point out, the preliminary drawings made by comics creators may be of legitimate interest to 'fans and researchers',[11] but they cannot be considered originals of the resulting comics, since the printed comic is the actual original. Importantly, this position is different from the question of whether comics artists' handmade works are original pieces of art. The unique configuration of the ideas and concepts that link the comics work to the processes and ideology of reproduction runs quite counter to the ideological functioning of facsimiles, which associate authenticity with an early or important (and visible, or visibly reproducible) version of a text. Comics, by contrast, associates only the provisional and the potential with the handwork of the author or artist: the drawn page is a stage in the pre-production of the comics work, even an important stage, but its authenticity does not and cannot supersede that of the published and reproduced comic itself.

So while comics works share both two-dimensionality and reproduction with photographic or other printed facsimiles, the two kinds of reproductions depart from one another in the nature of what it is they reproduce. Facsimiles, remediating editions, reproduce a stage (usually

---

[11] Abel and Madden, 'Foreword', p. vii.

an important stage or an authoritative stage) in the development of a text which is normally subject to the operation of an edition. A comics work, by contrast, literally produces something brand new as it reproduces: the reproduced comic is itself the result of an act of comics production, and vice versa. In this sense, the genre or medium of comics partakes of both the logic of production and of reproduction; one way of understanding the visibility of the artist's handiwork within comics is as a reflection of the nature of comics as multiplied simultaneous productions.

Comics works are not editions

If the refusal of comics to participate in remediation marks the degree to which comics works do not and cannot function as facsimiles, it remains necessary to show the degree to which comics works also fail, in the general case, to be editions. Although, like all texts or textual artefacts, comics can become the subject of editions, it shall be my contention in this section that, unlike printed books, where editions are the primary mode of articulation, comics do not normally function as editions.

Again, the claim seems both counterintuitive and manifestly wrong: the very logic I used above to suggest that comics works are texts seems also to suggest that comics works are reproduced in editions. That is, comics are texts because they are surrounded by a conventional series of paratexts (authorial names, titles, boundary-markers) and that those very same markers are the ones most frequently mobilized in editions, as discussed above in Chapter 3. Yet once again, the differences in the function of these paratexts reveal a crucial difference in effect.

In editions, as discussed above, paratexts are deployed to promise or to certify the authenticity, authority, or value of the text that the edition reproduces. The association of the author's name to the text is the most obvious paratextual mode of achieving this effect, but prefaces, notes, headings, page numbers, design, and many other sorts of paratextual strategies show the actions of editorial hands that are intended to assure and reassure readers of the value or authority of the text. But, of course, the value of the reproduced text is in need of such support because editions take the logic of copying as a defining factor: the printed text represents an ideal original that lies, conceptually, elsewhere than in the printed book.

In the case of comics, by contrast, there is no concept of any other original than the reproduced work itself.

Just as with the argument that comics works are not facsimiles, then, the argument that they are not editions also turns upon their lack of a prior or separate 'original'. What an edition of a comics work would need in order to function as an edition would be an ideal original, lying conceptually outside all printed manifestations of the work, that the edition could attempt to reproduce and (of course) fail at reproducing. But comics' refusal (in the general case) of typography makes such a possibility impossible. In typographical literary works, the novel or poem has a conceptual existence separate from its physical printings: the novel or poem or text is what does not (or should not) change when it is reset into a new typeface, or even a new setting of any sort. With comics, the prominence of hand-drawing and hand-lettering prevents the notion that a resetting can preserve the invisible core of the work, while altering the visible components that represent the work to readers. Where typography makes the printed, typographical work invisible and virtual (because the work itself is ideal, in the realm of ideas, and only a representation of the work can be seen via typography), comics works are irresistibly visible and real.

It is important to recognize that this understanding of comics does not deny the possibility that a printed work of comics might be flawed and in need of what is traditionally understood as editing. For example, in the copy of Alan Moore and Dave Gibbons's *Watchmen* that I own and read, Dr Manhattan's speech balloons occasionally lack the blue colouring they usually have.[12] I can, by the exercise of my own imagination, imagine a version of *Watchmen* in which this perceived flaw has been corrected, and it seems indeed to have been corrected in later printings of the book, although I have not yet determined when and where the production change was accomplished. But whether I imagine the corrected version, or Moore and Gibbons accomplished it, or DC editors did, it is always an act of imagination that brings the corrected form into being, not the nature of the printed comics medium. This is a crucial difference from typographical print, which (I argued in Chapter 3) invokes an ideal original as a part of the medium itself, regardless of whether any

---

[12] Alan Moore (writer) and Dave Gibbons (artist), *Watchmen* (New York: DC Comics, 1987), 3rd printing, ch. I, p. 22.

reader perceives flaws in a printed book. In comics, readers' application of Foucault's 'author function' (through its associated principles of coherence) is what generates the more ideal, more correct version, which may either be realized in a new printing or not.

To put it into other terms, a manifest failure of consistency in a comics work can still give rise to the effects and machinery of an edition, where such inconsistencies are ironed out, just as a new printing of *The Lord of the Rings* can make sure to use only 'elven' instead of 'elfin'. But the imagined or ideal 'more correct' (or 'more consistent') version of the comics work that operates in such cases differs ideologically from the imagined correct version of a typographic text, because the typographic text always insists upon the ideal version, while the comics text does not. The typographical text is understood to exist even before it is printed (for example, in manuscript or idea form), while the comics text literally does not exist until it is printed. For drawn works like comics, there can be no ideal original in the absence of a manifest inconsistency that can trigger the operation of the author function: the expression that a reader sees on a character's face cannot be compared to an imaginary, ideal, 'correct' expression. Far from being a minor point of difference between how comics and typographic texts behave, this difference amounts to a radically different orientation. Rather than having an ideal existence (again, an ideological existence in the realm of ideas) a comics work does not and cannot exist outside of its printings.

We should probably work out the implications of this radical difference a bit further. Does a later printing of *Watchmen* that makes all of Dr Manhattan's speech balloons blue become an 'edition' in the same way that a printed edition of *Beowulf* makes that poem into an edition? I believe not, because the cases are again significantly different. A 'corrected' version of *Watchmen* is exactly that, a corrected version, now existing (presumably) without any manifest inconsistency that might trigger the operation of the 'author function' by which such a (now hypothetical) inconsistency could be addressed. That is, the corrected printing becomes the real (emphatically not ideal) coherent text of the work, and its visible consistency and coherence now actually inhibit the reader's employment of any author function to locate authority outside the visible book. One may (and one may need to) edit a comics text, but what results still does not quite work like a conventional edition, especially if it is articulated without the implicit or explicit claims of authority or accuracy that define the printed edition in the first place. Certainly, the non-linguistic, drawn components of a comics work remain incompatible with an imagined or ideal 'correct' version of their drawn reality.

We might think through these issues by considering one particular page from Milt Gross's *He Done Her Wrong*. On the page I have in mind, the hero is being told by a travelling woodsman that the villain has checked into a hotel with the hero's love interest. The visible words 'Mr + Mrs' in the hotel register belie the book's promise to include no words, even while Gross uses a speech balloon with drawn images inside it to communicate the contents of the woodsman's speech visually. At the bottom of the image, however, we see a horizontal sequence of up-and-down pen-strokes, as if a caption had been overwritten or overdrawn; certainly, thinner lines can occasionally be seen lying under the broader strokes. No other image in the book has such a bottom edge, and it is hard not to see these strokes as marking over or marking out something that once was present and visible or legible. As such, the uniqueness of this image raises the possibility that it represents a textual inconsistency that can or must be resolved by recourse to an ideal original. But if this drawing once had a caption, it has been marked out; if the drawing once had a different bottom edge, it has been marked out. Thus, while the image may well show marks of authorial revision, it is equally clear that the author has allowed the image to stand as it is. Any desire we may have to 'read through' the marked out lines to find an underlying caption is literally an expression of our search for a hidden text, one imperfectly reflected in the printed edition. To read this image as part of a comics work, we must see and read what is there, and not trouble ourselves with what we cannot see. To worry about the artist's process of creation here is to ask about how Gross created the preliminary drawing, which is a different question from reading the comic itself. It is print that encourages us to see printed book and preliminary materials as both reflecting an ideal text; once again, however, comics are real, and there is no underlying ideal form.

But this line of thinking brings us back to the central issue: my discussion of printed editions in Chapter 3 suggested that the printed edition redeployed the paratextual apparatus of Gothic manuscripts as a mode of asserting the authority that editions require, the very authority that printed editions insistently locate in the ideal realm. In comics, as I have noted, many of the same paratexts reappear: authorial names, titles, well-articulated boundaries, and (often enough) prefaces of various sorts. But in comics, these paratexts must be disassociated from the prototypical print-edition function of articulating a link between the visible, printed text and its invisible, ideal, locus of textual authority, because there is no such ideal locus of authority for comics works. It may well be too early in the history of this new medium of comics to understand fully how or if the paratexts of the print-era edition will be redeployed and reconfigured in the future; in the following sections, however, I shall attempt to begin the work of understanding how such paratexts are already under revision in the hands of comics creators such as Art Spiegelman and Chris Ware, beginning with both authors' remarkable and surprising employment of typography.

Typography and paratext in Ware and Spiegelman

Art Spiegelman's *Maus* could hardly be a more consciously crafted production, as has now been extensively documented in the recently released *MetaMaus* book and DVD.[13] It is clearly a work of comics, and yet there may be reason to suppose that it is also, against the very grain of the comics medium, irresistibly characterized by at least some of the ideology that underwrites printed editions. That is, *Maus* makes notable and significant use of typography, as a central feature of its articulation, despite the ways in which *Maus* seems on the surface to relegate typography only to the paratexts.

A brief survey of *Maus [I]*'s employment of typographic elements, then, is in order, and we find typography on the spine, the front cover, the front flap of the 'French' wraps, the title page, the copyright/dedication page, the epigraph page, the contents page, the chapter titles, the bulk of the interior pages (in the form of page numbers), the final page, the rear 'French' flap, and the back cover.[14] Hardly a page of the first volume,

[13] Art Spiegelman, *MetaMaus* (New York: Pantheon 2011).
[14] It seems important to be clear on the multi-book nature of *Maus*: although first published serially in Spiegelman's *Raw* magazine, the first volume was printed as a trade paperback book in Art Spiegelman, *Maus: A Survivor's Tale* (New York: Pantheon, 1986); I will refer to this book as *Maus [I]*. The second volume was printed first as a hardcover, Art Spiegelman, *Maus A Survivor's Tale II: And Here My Troubles Began* (New York: Pantheon, 1991); I will refer to this book as *Maus II*. Also in 1991, the first volume was repackaged,

then, escapes the typographic component (the second volume is similar), and at first glance the general association between typography and paratext seems clear: the text of *Maus* is what is drawn, and the use of typography for paratextual materials would seem to reinforce that position, rather than to undermine it.

Yet this interpretation of the typographical element is surely insufficient, and the drawn images on the front and back covers of both volumes (like the printed endpapers of both *Maus I* and *Maus II*, which are drawn and non-typographic) surely should not be relegated to the category of mere 'paratext' lying outside the body of the text that is subject to reading and interpretation. The case can be made most clearly, I think, through a careful reading of the back covers of the *Maus* books. On both volumes of *Maus*, the back cover is dominated by a large map (of Poland on *Maus [I]* and *Maus I* and of Auschwitz on *Maus II*), each with an inset map (Rego Park, NY, on *Maus [I]* and *Maus I* and the Catskills on *Maus II*). On both large maps and insets, typography is used to indicate the identity of the places and structures shown, and the hand-drawn maps and their typographical components work together seamlessly: here, at least, the typographical component is not a mere paratextual appendage to the drawn map images. An ISBN number and a UPC barcode interrupt the map images on *Maus I* and *Maus II*, and surrounding typographical blurbs on both volumes also remind us of the marketing function of many paratexts; these features, too, discourage a reading of both maps as merely a part of the same paratextual baggage, precisely because of the way the more clearly paratextual materials surround and set off the maps.

But it is important to note that something more is going on with both maps: both explicitly and unmistakably borrow from the visual vocabulary of cheap American pocket-sized 'Dell mapback' paperbacks from the 1940s and 1950s. The maps (always placed on the rear cover) on Dell mapbacks frequently make use of both the large map/inset map dynamic and the boxed legends that we find on the back covers of Spiegelman's books. The sort of intertextual (or is it inter-paratextual?) visual quotation and referencing that characterizes Spiegelman's back-cover maps surely belongs in the realm of literary functionality, rather than mere

with some alterations, as Art Spiegelman, *Maus A Survivor's Tale I: My Father Bleeds History* (New York: Pantheon, 1986 [*recte* 1991]), in both trade paperback and hardcover editions. This third book I will refer to as *Maus I*.

paratextual addition: these maps are simultaneously comics in themselves, juxtaposing Europe and America in ways analogous to the narratives inside the books (as I will discuss more fully below), but also conceptually juxtapositioning the physical *Maus* books alongside the earlier Dell mapback tradition.[15] That is, if we understand these back-cover maps as paratexts, we might be inclined to understand their purpose as either to define the boundaries of the text, or to assert the authority of the surrounded text, or to market it. But the relation of Spiegelman's maps to those on the earlier Dell mapbacks (where the maps were indeed explicitly paratextual) involves a mode of meaning making that is textual, not paratextual, in its effects.

It is probably important to observe that, in this particular case, meaning is being produced from aspects of these physical books that complicate or undermine the very text/paratext splitting that underlies the functioning of printed, typographical editions. Of course, literary authors in the print era have long been undermining that very split themselves (as did Chaucer and Marie de France in the Gothic period), but Spiegelman's maps break down the text/paratext barrier by insisting on the physical integrity, unity, and coherence of the printed work of comics. These seeming paratexts are not serving the ends of an edition, centralizing the drawn component of *Maus* as 'the text'; rather they serve to remind us that the comics work does not have an 'original' other than its printed manifestation, and that all parts of that original, as a result, are integral parts of the whole. Since a printed copy of *Maus* is not an edition, all parts of the printed production are part of the work; Spiegelman's *Maus* books incorporate their paratexts into the body of the work (the body of the text) irresistibly, even while they seem on the surface to reify a text/paratext split through their use of drawn and typographic elements. That seeming paratexts are actually part of the text in the *Maus* books, however, can even be confirmed by a more careful consideration of Spiegelman's use of page numbering.

---

[15] It is probably worth noting that the interior artwork on the title page of *Maus [I]*, on the free endpaper of *Maus I*, and on the first interior page of *Maus II*, stands in each case as a black-and-white rendering of the cover artwork, in the 1991 volumes reduced in size and placed off-centre. 1950s Popular Library paperbacks, contemporary with Dell mapbacks, generally also featured reduced, black-and-white renderings of the cover artwork on the title page, and Spiegelman appears to be referencing earlier paperback publishing conventions here as well.

In *Maus [I]*, page numbers run sequentially from the first interior page (which is the book's title page) to the end: no interior page of *Maus [I]* stands outside the run of page numbers. A few pages, however, show no number: the title, copyright, and dedication pages, a blank (page [6]) and contents page (page [7]), and the final page, announcing *Maus II* as 'next'. Even the title pages of the various chapters have page numbers, although the blanks that generally precede or follow them do not. Three further times in the book, page numbers are missing: in the 'Prisoner on the Hell Planet' sequence; on page [147], where a large drawing of a mouse or rat occupies the space where the number would otherwise be; and on page [157], showing the entrance to Auschwitz with the drawing extended to the very cut edges of the page. What all three of these spots in *Maus [I]* indicate, of course, is that the page numbers do not appear on a part of the visible page that lies outside of the comics work itself: the numbers are typographical, but their presence or absence is, in fact, a part of the overall design of the page, and they therefore cannot be simply ignored as paratextual. The pages of *Maus [I]* do not serve to represent a hand-drawn original, surrounding a reproduction of that original with a frame that includes typographical page numbers; rather, as I suggested above, the pages *are* the original, and the typographical component is indeed a part of the text, as we might likewise conclude from the fact that the page numbers cover all the pages: even the copyright page is a page of the text here, just as we saw above in the case of Pynchon's *V.*, where the first edition also included all the 'preliminary' pages in the run of page numbers.

What goes for the page numbers and the back cover artwork, of course, must go also for the other parts of the *Maus* books that we might be inclined to label as paratext. Despite our familiarity with the workings of various paratexts within the print tradition, they cannot and do not function the same way within the comics tradition, in part because they appear to be irresistibly drawn into the realm of the text itself, and thus do not and cannot truly stand outside of it. Indeed, later printings such as *Maus I* shift around the order and effect of some of these ostensible paratexts, even including some new ones: but making such changes, I believe, makes the new book a new production, rather than merely a new edition of the same text. Such later printings or rearrangements occupy a contested position between how the text/paratext split operates in relation to printed works and how comics works pull items that the print tradition treats as paratexts right into the text—but of course this observation merely reveals how necessary it becomes to understand how typographical print and comics articulate the nature of texts and paratexts differently at a fundamental level.

If my examination of Spiegelman's *Maus* books does not make the case sufficiently, the comics productions of Chris Ware can hardly be understood in any other fashion. Ware's works repeatedly and relentlessly demolish any hypothetical distinction between their textual component and what might be imagined or understood as their accompanying paratexts. Indeed, one hardly even knows where to begin, when confronted by the hardback first edition of Ware's best-known book, *Jimmy Corrigan: The Smartest Kid on Earth.*[16] The title, publisher, and author's name ('Mr F. C. Ware') are, indeed, present on the dust jacket spine, although partly inverted. All three are also present on the spine of the book proper. On both jacket and spine, these items are hand-lettered or drawn, rather than typographic, hinting that they are integral components of the comics text, not external paratexts. The dust jacket unfolds into a large, two-sided comics poster, partly typographic and partly comics-diagrammatic, including content found nowhere else within the book. The front endpapers include a typographic set of 'General Instructions' for reading comics (including a multiple-choice exam), an incredibly dense diagrammatic model of how comics work, and a brief typographic essay entitled 'New Pictorial Language Makes Marks'.[17] The next page shows a drawn field of stars, and the traditional 'comics' component of the book is off and running.[18] There is no clear title page, although the title words 'Jimmy Corrigan: The Smartest Kid on Earth' are repeated in various graphic configurations three times on the eighth page, and twice more on the ninth, where the Library of Congress Cataloguing-in-Publication information is found, again drawn by hand rather than typeset. Surrounding all of these items, however, are the

---

[16] Chris Ware, *Jimmy Corrigan: The Smartest Kid on Earth* (New York: Pantheon, 2000), 3rd printing.

[17] On Ware's use of diagrams, see Isaac Cates, 'Comics and the Grammar of Diagrams', in David M. Ball and Martha B. Kuhlman, eds., *The Comics of Chris Ware: Drawing is a Way of Thinking* (Jackson: University Press of Mississippi, 2010), pp. 90–104.

[18] In the following page references, I count this page of stars as the first page of the book proper, though doing so runs against the convention of identifying rectos as odd-numbered pages; see below.

panels of the continuing narration, and other title-like graphics are spread right throughout the book. On the fourteenth page, another title is found, this time with printing and copyright information, with different drawn text for various printings; the third printing reads 'This is the third edition, and hopefully reflects a marked improvement in appearance over the first two; the author was present at its printing.'[19] The copyright holder is identified as 'Mr Chris Ware'.[20] Throughout the book, the pages are unnumbered (except for pages 206–7, where 206 is clearly a recto, in contrast to the more usual convention). The rear endpapers are labelled as containing 'Corrigenda' (punning on the main character's name), and unlike the front endpapers, they are drawn, not typeset; the author's name is given here as 'Ware, C.'[21]

As even such a whirlwind summary suggests, there is not a single page of the book (nor even any aspect of its external appearance, including both sides of the dust jacket) that can be safely excluded from the book's text: any and all paratexts, even the most seemingly mechanical ones, like the copyright information and the Library of Congress Cataloguing-in-Publication notice, are absorbed into the hand-drawn portions of the main text, and the typographic components of both book and dust jacket clearly involve textual elements, rather than paratextual ones. Even the author's name is not deployed as a guarantor of coherence or authority: each of the three times it appears, the author's name is given differently. In typical Chris Ware fashion, the drawn words that make up the bulk of the linguistic component of *Jimmy Corrigan* are often drawn so precisely and regularly as to be almost visually indistinguishable from typography. In this sense, *Jimmy Corrigan* blurs the boundary between typography and hand-drawing as insistently and thoroughly as it refuses to distinguish between textual and paratextual components or apparatuses.

Also like *Maus*, when *Jimmy Corrigan* was reprinted, in paperback format, it had a full set of new seeming-paratexts attached: brand new wrap-around artwork for the covers, interior pages featuring selections from reviews (presented typographically) juxtaposed to a greatly reduced version of the artwork that first appeared on the interior of the

[19] Ware, *Jimmy Corrigan*, 3rd printing, n.n.
[20] Ware, *Jimmy Corrigan*, 3rd printing, n.n.
[21] Ware, *Jimmy Corrigan*, 3rd printing, rear pastedown.

hardcover's dust jacket, and new hand-drawn words for the copyright/
title page, still located thirteen pages in from the field-of-stars page.[22]
But lest we mistake these changes as being mere paratextual changes, a
new two-page drawn comics passage is also added in after the 'Corrigenda', and this passage really cannot be read as paratext. The new,
paperback printing of *Jimmy Corrigan*, we must conclude is, in fact, the
production of a new comic, one which overlaps a great deal with the
hardcover versions, but which nevertheless is a different work, with a
different text at a number of levels, including a different ending or post-
script.[23] Calling the paperback a 'paperback edition', notably, somewhat
misrepresents the way in which the paperback printing is indeed a
(slightly) different work, a new original. But the varying drawn texts on
the copyright/title pages of the various hardcover printings had already
pointed in the same direction, of course. Although we, as readers, might
choose or wish to identify one particular production of *Jimmy Corrigan*
(such as the first edition, or the original serial printings as volumes of
The Acme Novelty Library) as especially authoritative and definitive, the
reality is that the differences in the various printings and editions are not
consonant with a position that sees them as varying versions or representations of an ideal original that remains essentially unchanged. The
differences between the various printings simply cannot be understood
as failures of editing or failures of reproduction, and these real differences cannot be regularized by imagining a controlling or authoritative
ideal version.

What the examples of *Maus* and *Jimmy Corrigan* teach us, then, is
that—for the moment at least—the unique nature of comics books and
comics texts leaves no room at all for paratextual material that lies outside of the text, in part because (as Abel and Madden observed) the
original printing of a comics work is the simultaneous moment of its

---

[22] Chris Ware, *Jimmy Corrigan: The Smartest Kid on Earth* (New York: Pantheon, 2003),
4th paperback printing. Notably, the insertion of the two pages of review-quotations
changes the implied pagination of the book, although the pages labelled 'Pages 206–7' in
both printings are the same, suggesting that the new review-quotation pages might best
be numbered [i–ii]. Of course, the inclusion of the complex comics diagram, and not
merely reviews, undermines the attempt to identify these pages as paratext pages which
might be suitably numbered with Roman numerals.

[23] Similarly, of course, the initial hardcover printing of *Jimmy Corrigan* is different in
various ways from the earlier printing of similar material in various volumes of Ware's
series *The Acme Novelty Library*.

production and its reproduction. In contrast to Gothic reproduction and print reproduction, both of which articulated themselves in part through the very splitting of text and paratext, comics production (we might call it rather comics reproduction, as it is both) refuses such a split entirely. As in the Anglo-Saxon period, when manuscripts might occupy a position either within an economy of production or an economy of reproduction, the twentieth and twenty-first centuries are clearly a time when at least two modes operate simultaneously. But it is clear also that comics, which might seem on the surface to be a mere formal variation on textuality, also represent a mode of production-in-reproduction that is essentially new on the scene, and configured innovatively in comparison to prior forms and modes.

It shall remain to be seen, I suspect, whether or not this mode of paratextless production-in-reproduction will continue to dominate comics in the long term, although one way to understand what I have been describing is yet another reconfiguration of the purpose and effect of paratextuality—here, its actual incorporation into textuality itself. But simultaneously, the thoroughgoing incorporation of paratexts into comics texts highlights the radical materiality of comics textuality: because they are not merely different editions, *Maus [I]* and *Maus I* are different texts, different literary works, just as the various hardback and paperback and serial printings of *Jimmy Corrigan* are different works. Part of comics' resistance to the ideology of print lies in comics' challenge to the notion that 'the text' is ideal, imaginary, linguistic, irreal: comics are real, and their material component is always part of both what comics are and what comics mean.

The hands of the authors

One remarkable feature of Spiegelman's back cover maps is the degree to which they differ stylistically (in their use of colour, in their use of typography within the images, and in other ways) from the drawn images that make up the bulk of the *Maus* books. As if to highlight the contrast, both back covers also include an image of Vladek Spiegelman (and, in one case, Artie) drawn in the same fashion as the interior artwork. These drawings of Vladek generally stand in front of and overlap the maps; the map on the back of *Maus II* also includes a drawing of a black column of smoke rising from the crematorium smokestack. The overlap effect is striking: in front of or on top of the maps of Poland, we see maps of New York, and (especially on *Maus II*) foregrounded in relation to both of those layers are drawings in the style of the drawings in the interior of the book: Vladek in an Auschwitz uniform, or Vladek's house in Rego Park. Much more directly than the full-colour artwork on the front covers of the *Maus* books, then, these foregrounded drawings on the maps function as 'vestibules' or entryways into the 'text', in classic Genette-style paratextual fashion, as they lead us from the colourful exteriors of the book towards the monochrome interior-style artwork.

Yet given my arguments above about how Spiegelman reconfigures all seeming paratexts into the text component of these books, I should probably rephrase that conclusion. The stylistic similarity of these fore-grounded black-and-white drawings eases the reader's transition from full-colour covers to black-and-white interior. But such easing is accom-plished through the apparent layering of visually complementary aspects of what is, on each back cover, a single coherent composition: the vesti-bule effect that Genette identifies for paratexts is clearly being mobilized, but it is also clear that it here ties together two separate domains of the text, rather than serving to distinguish textual interior from exterior.

We might come at the issue from a somewhat different angle and note that the layered effect of the map covers serves to position the largest geography ('*Poland*,' on *Maus [I]*; '*Poland 1944*' on *Maus II*) as the bot-tom or fundamental layer. Superimposed on these larger maps are smaller, yellowish maps (bordered by red) showing the Catskills or Rego Park, New York. Within or in front of these inset maps are images of Vladek or his house in Rego Park, drawn in the black-and-white style of the books' interiors. The back covers thus explicitly articulate Vladek's story, as narrated in the *Maus* books, in relationship to both the broader geography of Poland and the somewhat narrower geography of New York. In this sense, the back cover maps take their places as part of the 'reflexive ethnography' effect of the *Maus* books recently discussed by Rosemary Hathaway.[24] Further, the back cover maps explicitly reference

---

[24] Rosemary Hathaway, 'Reading Art Spiegelman's *Maus* as Postmodern Ethnography', *Journal of Folklore Research* 48.3 (2011), 249–67. That the black-and white image on the back cover of *Maus [I]* and *Maus I* shows Artie listening at Vladek's knee specifically emphasizes the enthographic collection of Vladek's story.

two of the most famous and widely discussed images from inside the books: the plume of smoke from the crematorium on the back of *Maus II* echoes the smoke from Artie's cigarette that rises as if from the crematorium chimney on page 69 of *Maus II*, while both maps subtly evoke the image of the Polish landscape showing roads in the shape of a swastika on page 125 of the first volume. The stylistic visual reference to the interior narrative is compounded or reinforced by the content-based references in a way that must be read as a mode of literary reference, rather than intertextual reference. Here, too, the maps are part of the texts, rather than separate texts or paratexts.

But the various styles employed on the covers of the *Maus* books belie the remarkable coherence and consistency of style which is seen on the interiors (with the exception of the 'Prisoner on the Hell Planet' sequence). Maintained with notable consistency over the twelve years (from 1980 to 1991) of the original serial publication of *Maus*, Spiegelman's style gives the appearance of a hastily drawn, even rough composition. This visual effect is plainly intentional, and Spiegelman's comments about his stylistic intentions as they now appear in *MetaMaus* are incredibly revealing:

> I decided to work same size as publication: the drawings that you see in the book are in exactly a one-to-one ratio to the size they're drawn. It affords a degree of intimacy, an 'I-thou' kind of moment that doesn't allow me to take refuge in the minimizing of one's hand tremor.... Reproducing one's own mark—offering up a facsimile of one's own handwriting—makes it more like looking into an actual journal.... Using stationery store supplies, bond paper, typewriter correction fluid, and a fountain pen made it more like writing, like offering up a manuscript, something made by hand.[25]

In the context of my own argument, Spiegelman's insistence on terms like 'manuscript', 'journal', 'facsimile', and 'reproducing' serve to call attention to the ways in which Spiegleman recognizes that the work of comics he has produced focuses readers' attention on the personal aspect of what they read. Built into *Maus* at every level is a conscious attempt to make the reproduction (of at least the interior pages of *Maus*) seem as much as possible like a singular, hand-made production: the size,

---

[25] Spiegelman, *MetaMaus*, p. 174.

materials, and style of drawing all work together to achieve those artistic ends. Among the many remarkable formal accomplishments of *Maus* is this almost perfect match between what Spiegelman intends and the nature of comics works themselves as simultaneous productions and reproductions.

To put it in other terms, Spiegelman uses a fountain pen and type-writer correction fluid not because those features will indeed be repro-duced (they will not) but in order to give the (reproduced/produced) work that results from the use of those tools the feel of 'the real', rather than the feel of the simulacrum. Spiegelman's visual stylistic choices, in *Maus*, work with and work within an understanding of comics as real, and not representational, at their core. If one says nothing else about *Maus*, one must note that Spiegelman's widely discussed decision to use drawings of mice instead of drawings of people is strikingly non-representational in exactly the way that a comics book is a thing, rather than a printed representation of a text that has its central ideological location elsewhere.[26] If Spiegelman draws himself and other characters as humans, the issue of representational accuracy is raised in a way that is obviated by his use of mice; although the use of mice is surely an inspired choice, its most important aspect may be that Spiegelman is not drawing humans. The 'real', journal-like feeling Spiegelman is striving for and the non-representational character of his mouse metaphor are both aspects of the way in which *Maus* is built as a comics production-in-reproduction.

Interestingly, Spiegelman's efforts to use a personal, seemingly unre-fined drawing style, as well as one-to-one reproduction size and black-and-white presentation, are opposed, in each case, by the stylistic choices that generally characterize Chris Ware's work. Ware's typical style is both highly refined, precise, and usually somewhat abstract, with both draw-ing and lettering that strike the eye as almost mechanical and even typo-graphic. In part this effect is, indeed, achieved by Ware's use of reproductive reductions in size. But also, Ware generally makes thor-ough, and often remarkable, use of colour, added to his drawings during the reproductive process through computer mediation, and thus literally

---

[26] The three central questions Spiegelman uses *MetaMaus* to address are 'Why the Holocaust?', 'Why Mice?', and 'Why Comics?', with lengthy chapters under each of these titles.

not the product of handwork. In these differences, Ware serves as a remarkable foil for Spiegelman's work in *Maus*, and yet Ware, too, is clearly concerned to make artistic and literary use of the most central defining aspects of the comics form.

Despite their manifest differences, Ware's style is every bit as individual and recognizable as Spiegelman's, and in that sense, style is a marker of authorial identity for both. Instead of the feel of a personal journal, Ware strives to achieve something else, often seeming to invoke the feel of comics from an earlier age: his comics often adapt or borrow the visual vocabulary of Frank King's 'Gasoline Alley' strips, or early twentieth-century advertising, or archaic ephemeral toys such as cut-out paper models.[27] Indeed, in their intertextual referencing of antecedent aspects of popular visual (and textual) culture, Ware and Spiegelman are sometimes more alike than different, although their references are usually accomplished through different stylistic means. But the very differences point up the more compelling and revealing underlying similarities: Ware's works, too, not only insist on the absence of a meaningful text/paratext split, but they also make the physical materiality of the work into an active component of meaning.

I can hardly do better than to call attention once again to an aspect of *Jimmy Corrigan* that I have discussed elsewhere, the model of Jimmy's grandmother's house on pages 206–7 of the book.[28] On these pages (and in numerous analogous pages, both in *Jimmy Corrigan* and in the *Acme Novelty Library* and in *Quimby the Mouse*), Ware presents readers with paper models that might be cut out and assembled into actual structures, often enough with working moving parts. Ware's style, with its precise lines, smooth curves, even colouring, and occasional incorporation of typography, even allows a surprising degree of visual continuity between the cut-outs and the ongoing narrative. Readers of these cut-out pages, of course, must either actually cut these books apart or imagine doing so (in the case of the grandmother's house, the act must remain imaginary, as the cut-outs are printed on both sides of a single leaf). Even contemplating

[27] See Jeet Heer, 'Inventing Cartooning Ancestors: Ware and the Comics Canon', in David M. Ball and Martha B. Kuhlman, eds., *The Comics of Chris Ware: Drawing is a Way of Thinking* (Jackson: University Press of Mississippi, 2010), pp. 3–13, and Daniel Raeburn, 'Building a Language', in Daniel Raeburn, *Chris Ware* (New Haven: Yale University Press, 2004), pp. 6–26.

[28] Bredehoft, 'Comics Architecture, Multidimensionality, and Time'.

the destruction of the physical book, however, calls our attention to its physicality in a surprisingly direct fashion, and the way in which Ware makes such a contemplation serve as part of the reader's experience of the text insists that the physical book is the locus of textual meaning and meaning-making. Although the house we build from the cut-out plans may remain in our imagination, this use of imagination is not a matter of comparing the text we read to an ideal form; to say so, of course, merely repeats the conclusion above that the comics work is not an edition.

Elsewhere, Ware confronts readers with the physicality and materiality of his works through variations of size and scale. The *Quimby the Mouse* and *Acme Novelty Library* books are each over fourteen inches tall, and their pages are sometimes filled with type (or comics panels) so small as to be practically unreadable.[29] We might, of course, compare Spiegelman's *In the Shadow of No Towers*, which is also printed as a very large book indeed.[30] But Ware also has sometimes presented comics works in incredibly small formats, and the continuing experimentation with the shape, size, and form of printed comics works is an essential component of Ware's *Acme Novelty Library* series.[31] That this series also plays with the printing and publishing conventions regarding title pages, copyright pages, and other 'paratextual' components reveals the degree to which Ware's recurring concerns make linkages between the physical, material aspects of comics production, on the one hand, and the impossibly of distinguishing text from paratext in comics works, on the other.

Though their styles could hardly be more different, then, Spiegelman and Ware appear to be responding to a remarkably similar set of formal concerns that serve to define comics reproduction itself. What they teach us about comics is that comics exists paradigmatically as a kind of text defined by production-in-reproduction. To the degree that comics works irresistibly draw paratexts into the text and to the degree that they operate as real, material entities uncontrolled by an ideal original, comics works are texts that serve a different reproductive logic than typographically printed texts (and their ideological descendants) do. These

---

[29] Chris Ware, *The Acme Novelty Library Final Report to Shareholders* (New York: Pantheon, 2005).

[30] Art Spiegelman, *In the Shadow of No Towers* (New York: Pantheon, 2004).

[31] See the tiny comics, 'many of which are no larger than a thumbnail', in Ware's curio cabinet, shown in Raeburn, *Chris Ware*, p. 50.

authors are beginning the work of incorporating these formal and ideological innovations into their works, and where the genre of comics is
ultimately headed may not yet be either clear or fully determined. But
the importance of comics, as a mode of textual reproduction that
operates on a different ideological basis from typographic print, can
hardly be overstated, especially at a moment when scholars (and the
general public) are so highly focused on the emerging domain of digital
reproduction.

Conclusions

Perhaps the most remarkable and surprising claim made in this chapter
is that the mode of ideological working identified here as typical of comics also operates whenever two-dimensional images or structures play a
meaningful role *within* the text, as opposed to merely serving paratextual ends. That is, although many illustrations and other two-dimensional
structures may indeed serve only as paratexts, not all do, and whenever
two-dimensional juxtapositions operate as part of the reproduced text
itself we have entered the realm of comics. And while comics has only
come into prominence as a literary from, a form suited to imaginative
literature, in the last century or so, the long histories of argument-
via-diagram, intentionally ironic illustration, and various other textual
strategies remind us that the comics mode has a history virtually as long
as the history of print itself. Understanding comics demands, I believe, a
re-evaluation of the nature and history of print itself, because print has
virtually always included a non-typographic component, even if we have
often focused on typography as the defining aspect of print.

Specifically, Chris Ware's play with diagrammatic comics, cut-out
paper models, and ephemeral paper art from the early twentieth century
serves to reference a history of two-dimensional structures of meaning
in print that have long undermined print's defining ideology of textual
linearity. Spiegelman's equal fascination with historical precursors, both
in *In the Shadow of No Towers*, where he explores and evokes early twentieth-century comics, and in the swiping of the notion of 'mapback'
cover artwork on the *Maus* volumes, highlights how both artists draw
inspiration from a range of sources that lie outside the mainstream of
what literary scholars understand as the textual genealogy of literature.

Spiegelman and Ware point us towards an alternative tradition of print, one in which typography cannot impose its linearity.

What comics can teach us, then, is to attend to the heretofore hidden or unregarded history of two-dimensional meaning-making strategies as articulating a response to the central ideologies of print, those which define the nature of the literary work as linear and linguistic, as being possessed of an ideal form imperfectly reflected in written or printed copies, as defined and articulated through the machinery of the edition and its mobilization of paratexts. Each in their own ways, the literary comics works I have considered most closely in this chapter, by Gross, Spiegelman, and Ware, all work to undermine the machinery of the edition, in the ways in which they subsume paratext into text, blur the boundaries between typography and illustration, and insist upon the originality of the printed artefact itself as the only locus of authority. These literary authors are, of course, engaged in play, but of the very kind of play we see on the Franks Casket, in Chaucer, in More's *Utopia*, and in Tolkien's *Lord of the Rings* Appendices: the play with, and against, the very boundaries of the defining paradigms in which literary creation occurs.

Epilogue

Virtually every word I have written in this book has been written virtually: composed on a computer, taking its primary existence as a sequence of tiny, invisible electromagnetic data points, and being made visible (or not) by the workings of a screen or printer. Occasionally, of course, I have also hand-written corrections or revisions on a hard-copy printout, although such corrections cannot really join my text until they, too, are entered via keyboard. These dynamics remind us, of course, that many of us now inhabit a world where digital text, hard-copy printed text, and hand-written manuscript all play a role in our species of textuality.

So one of the things I wish to do, in rounding out this current project, is to remind my own readers of the degree to which this state of affairs may not be as new or unusual as it sometimes seems. Multiple technologies and ideologies of text and textuality have been operative in every period of my study: both Anglo-Saxon and Gothic periods had both productive and reproductive ideologies, though they seem to have been differently valued (and also somewhat differently configured) in the two periods. Nor could print entirely eliminate either manuscript writing or the idea of a truly singular production. Likewise, my suggestion in Chapter 4 that two-dimensional comics-like structures of meaning have a history almost as long as the history of print itself serves to remind us that not all print is typographic, and that print itself is a more complex phenomenon than the focus on typography allows, even while the very ideology of print urges us to focus on typography and its associated linearity. To the degree that print mobilizes the notion of an ideal text, print itself seems to open the door to an understanding of text as virtual: indeed, 'virtual' as a descriptive term probably suits the ideal text lying behind print better than it does the physical text encoded in electronic circuitry.[1]

From the sort of perspective I have developed here, what is remarkable and innovative about digital text is not its supposed 'virtuality' but rather the invisibility or unseeability of its physical manifestations. Virtual text is, of course, quite real indeed: a matter of electrons and magnetic states and so on. And when we route it to a printer, it becomes real in another sense, as ink on paper. Only when it appears on the screen do we treat it as if it were ephemeral, somehow, evanescent and always in danger of vanishing. But the truth is, like other real texts, digital text is as robust as its writing support: although computers do occasionally crash and destroy texts, so too do blackboards get erased, inks fade, and papers burn.

In terms of its reliance upon its writing support, it seems to me crucial to acknowledge that the nature of digital text is, if anything, even more relentlessly linear than printed text. Whether I am contemplating a Microsoft Word file, a pdf, an HTML file, or an XML file, it remains essentially a single, linear sequence of digital bits and bytes. Even digitized pictures are stored electronically as linear sequences of data, though coded to be presented in two dimensions. The two-dimensional display of linear, digitized texts and images, it appears, must be understood as a kind of reproduction, even as the process of (linearly) copying a computer file (say, from a thumbdrive to a hard drive, or during a download from the Web) is also a kind of reproduction. What digital text involves is a crucial bifurcation of reproduction: digital reproduction involves both machine-readable reproduction, ordered linearly, and demanding strictly linearized text, and human-readable reproduction, on screen or in hard-copy, involving a display protocol that allows the linear text to be displayed in two dimensions. In order to understand textual reproduction in the digital domain, we must constantly attend to which of these two modes of reproduction occupies our attention at any point.

---

[1] 'Virtual' ought to mean 'without a physical presence'; electronic text, of course, does have a physical presence, so printed text depends upon an imagined 'virtual' text more straightforwardly than does electronic text.

But what we should never forget, I think, is the degree to which the act of digitizing privileges those parts of texts, images, and books that are susceptible to linearization. Scanning (and displaying) texts or images with higher and higher degrees of resolution may involve exciting technological innovations, but digitization remains a technology strikingly akin to typography. If the ideological effect of typography was, as I argued in Chapter 3, to bring to prominence an ideal understanding of textual identity and definition, digitization seems likely to have a similar effect: we will come to understand or believe that 'the text' is that component of a work (or file) which remains (or ought to remain) unchanged, regardless of what display protocol is used to render it visible to us. Implicit in digital text, I believe, is the notion that display protocols will indeed render texts visible in multiple ways, and that readers' experiences of digital texts may well vary more widely than even their visual experiences of printed books.

It may be difficult, however, to tell what is at stake in such a possibility without considering a concrete example, and probably the most familiar sort of visual modification we see in digital text centres on size. Readers of digital text (whether they read through a web browser, on a word processor, or on a reader such as a Kindle) almost always have the ability to increase or decrease the size of the characters they read, and image processing software likewise makes zooming in or out of images a matter of just a few mouse-clicks or the like. These changes, based in the display protocols that make the digital text visible, already are understood as not changing 'the text,' in part because of a lingering analogy from the era of typographic print, where the size of printed letters was understood to have no impact on the text itself. But the logic is clear: we tend to think that the size of reproduction is irrelevant in relation to digital texts, because the text itself is understood to be linear.

In this sense, comics works, which (as I discussed in Chapter 4) depend upon their very two-dimensionality at a definitional level, cannot really be accommodated into the realm of digital text, because digitization demands linearity as thoroughly as the comics form demands two dimensions. That is, while a comics work must be drawn in two dimensions, and can indeed be digitized by scanning, and even published on the web with no paper publication, the display protocols for images make size variable and adjustable for digitized comics works, if by no other means that by our ability to read them on screens of various sizes. Printed comics works, always made real by the process of production-in-reproduction, always have a physical size, and that size is literally one aspect of the meaning-making experience of reading, as Spiegelman's intentions regarding the one-to-one size reproduction of *Maus* pages will confirm. Webcomics, interesting as they no doubt are, are not really comics in this sense, as webcomics are variable in size as a consequence of their very digitization. Though no conceivable human reading or display protocol can truly dispense with a digital comics work's two-dimensionality, its variability in size is nothing less than a consequence of the linearity of the underlying real electronic 'text-as-digital-representation'.

Again, it may be too early in the history of digital text to fully understand the implications of the new mode of linearization allowed or enforced by digital technology, but it should be clear that the size of what we see or read is newly variable in the digital realm, and that this dynamic discourages any focus on the materiality of digital text. Indeed, where printed books always opened the door for materialist and two- or three-dimensional readings, the display protocols for digital text (at least at the moment) focus on two-dimensionality at the expense of materiality. Although it is manifestly untrue, digital text (like print) pretends that text is ultimately immaterial, and thus available for reproduction in various modes that explicitly always reshape it.

In its focus on linearity and an ideal, immaterial underlying text subject to reproduction, digital reproduction remains very closely tied to the ideology of typographic print. Yet it may be the case (and again, I suspect it is too early to be sure) that the display protocols employed for digital texts may resist the logic of the copy. Where typographic print (but not comics print) takes the logic of the copy as a given (printed copies always fail at representing the text, which is ideal), digital text encourages us to trust the display protocols in a way we might not trust the underlying text. To put it in other terms, while the material digital text may still have an error, typo, or other flaw, and we may well feel that the actual electronic form of the text is in need of revision or correction, we take it as a matter of faith (the ideology of digital textuality) that the display protocols that make it visible to us are transparent and immediate. The digital bifurcation of reproduction into machine-copying and visible display seems (at the moment, at least) to split into two domains: the physical, electronic text remains subject to the logic of the copy, as physical, printed, typographic texts always were, while the reproduction involved in visible display is held to be innocent of the logic of the copy.

Nowhere is this dynamic more apparent, I suspect, than in the production and consumption of digital facsimiles, whether reproductions of art, printed books, or medieval manuscripts. In its physical form, a digital facsimile is, of course, nothing but a series of electronic states, standing (in their essential difference from one another) for conceptual ones and zeroes, stored on some device somewhere as a linearly organized file. When properly displayed, of course, such files look very much indeed like the objects from which they derive, and while we may worry or wonder about the quality, resolution, or accuracy of the scan (worries about the quality of the underlying physical file, and whether or not it represents the physical original accurately), I suspect few of us worry that the display protocol is equally subject to the logic of the copy. That is, if we worry about the logic of the copy in relation to the digital facsimile, we focus that anxiety on the quality of the physical file (as a potential failure of reproduction) but not on the additional reproduction of the display protocol, which we understand as a successful representation of the physical file. That is, if we zoom into an image so far that the resolution gets blocky, we blame the quality of the scan, not the limitations of our display protocol.

If we step outside of that ideology, however, it appears to be clear that display protocols that allow us to see digital images on screens and to print them on paper must have their own weaknesses and blindspots. Perhaps not every aspect of an original work or item can be shown or seen on a two-dimensional screen or printed surface. Or perhaps size really does matter, as I suggested above was always the case in comics works. Or, as I argued is the case for many Anglo-Saxon manuscripts, perhaps the very notion of reproduction transforms the nature of the artefact, which may properly be a production and thus should be encountered directly, without the mediation of reproduction.

The point that I am really trying to make, of course, is that the production of digital texts involves a textual ideology that is no more innocent in its effects and consequences than the ideologies explored in the four periods or domains covered in my first four chapters. And if I understand it, the new ideology is one that splits digital reproduction into a two-stage process. On the one hand, we have the machine-reproduction of digital texts, which is subject to the logic of the copy and involves an

ideal, immaterial text. On the other hand, we have the secondary reproduction performed by digital display protocols, which is held to be
transparent and immediate, a perception reinforced every time I strike
a key and the corresponding character appears on my screen as if
instantaneously.

Perhaps I should pursue the implications of this line of logic one tiny
step further: the display protocols we treat as transparent in this ideological argument are, indeed, themselves nothing but linear sequences
of electronic bits. The bifurcation of reproduction which I have been trying to trace appears to insist upon a crucial distinction between digital
text and digital programming, which I suspect is indeed configured differently from paratext. This distinction may well prove to be the defining
feature of digital technology.

Then again, it may not, for reasons that are intimately connected to
my hesitation in believing that the era of digital technology is sufficiently
far along to give us any clear sense of what ideology it will ultimately
drive (or vice versa). The fact of the matter is that there appears to already
be a thriving area of digital culture which indeed refuses the distinction
between 'text' and 'programming' as thoroughly as comics or the Ellesmere Chaucer refuses or complicates a distinction between text and
paratext. But whether we consider hypertext or digital gaming, the experience of reading or experiencing the digital 'text' (again, via various display protocols) is the experience of engaging with programming in
addition to construing bits of written language or displays of two-
dimensional images. But these issues, fascinating as they are, can only
be briefly approached here, and my comments can barely scratch the
surface or indicate some trends and possibilities.

Large or small, narrative digital games and hypertexts remain, essentially, linearly coded digital texts: all of Wikipedia is stored somewhere
as a series of linearly organized textual objects. Yet, like virtually any
single-player narrative digital game, Wikipedia has no single, canonical,
defining structural or architectural sequence through which a reader is
expected to pass. That is, linearly organized texts from any prior period
or domain generally do have a structuring architecture, even if readers
have always had the option to read non-sequentially—because flipping
to the end of a mystery novel does nothing to actually alter the structure
of the novel itself. Whether we focus on reader/player interactivity or on
the nature of the programming, programming-based digital text allows

multiple paths for readers, without structuring any single path as canonical. When we make a choice in a game, or click a link in a hypertext, what we see, read, and experience shifts or alters due to the programming. And it shifts in such a way as to undermine any clear distinction between text and programming.

The result is incredibly disorienting from the perspectives of conventional textuality: digital texts that operate in this fashion, including a huge spectrum of hypertexts and games, have no structure in the conventional sense, and virtually any two readers of these works will have different experiences, and they will very probably not see or read the same words and images. A hypertext like Wikipedia has no beginning or end (just as it has no clear boundaries, as it includes external links); a game probably does have at least one beginning, but it may have no end, one end, or a variety of ends, and the game itself is something different from any individual session of play. In that sense, individual play sessions may have ends or endings, but the game itself may not.

But it is important to see that the issues are not limited to these types of examples: to the degree that digital editions of medieval texts and manuscripts take the form of hypertexts, they too are already showing the results of the digital breakdown between text and programming: digital hypertextual editions become a web of clickable links with some artefact or text nominally at the centre, but the very integration of text and programming inherent in hypertext at least potentially undermines the effort to place one text at the centre of the hypertextual web. The structure of a hypertext has no true centre, as it has no beginning and end, and any effort to reinforce a text/paratext split within a hypertext web is, in one sense, a failure of remediation: the attempt to reproduce a feature of an older medium in the medium actually being used. But the degree to which hypertexts threaten the text/paratext split while comics also undermine it seems to me to suggest that the text/paratext boundary may currently be under greater pressure than at any point in the past.

Perhaps the central point this book has made is the observation that media are not technologies, but technologies as they are associated with ideologies of reproduction; my other contribution, I hope, has been to trace some of the specific conjunctions of technology and ideology that have been operative across the history of English literature. Seen from such a perspective, Anglo-Saxon manuscripts differ in their function from Gothic manuscripts because the ideologies differ, but not the technologies. Likewise, typographical print and comics print differ ideologically, while both rely upon the basic technology of the printing press itself. Digital technology is crucially important as a new mode of reproduction, but what ideology or ideologies will ultimately configure it seems difficult to guess at this point. What does seem clear, however, is that the business of making editions, to the degree that it derives from (and ideologically invokes) the medium of typographic print (with all that it entails), engages in remediation differently for works from the Anglo-Saxon period, the Gothic period, or from the world of comics-style two-dimensionality. And to the degree that electronic editions of even printed texts also involve a sort of remediation, we inhabit a moment when the practices and ideas underlying the edition, which seem so very natural and inevitable to those of us raised upon editions, is undergoing a kind of radical rupture.

Further, our foundational practices of textual criticism, based as they are upon a print-oriented understanding that 'the text' exists as an ideal, perfect, linguistic structure, are thoroughly incompatible with the ideologies of the Anglo-Saxon, Gothic, and comics domains. Making editions, of course, remains valuable work, and I have no wish to undervalue such work, but I do believe we have a responsibility to acknowledge and address the ways in which editions quite literally remake texts and textual artefacts into the image of print-based textuality. We must learn to read these other textual objects in their own terms, and we might also find it necessary to rethink our practices of editing. Importantly, the moment is ripe to reconceptualize editing and textual criticism not only because digital editions involve new ideologies and new opportunities, but also because we can now more accurately identify the ideologies that structure early texts more precisely.

For Anglo-Saxon textual productions like *Beowulf* or *The Dream of the Rood*, we must attend more carefully to the implications of how these productions operated in their original context outside of any ideology of reproduction. As productions or artefacts that do not inherently invoke an underlying ideal textual original, these Anglo-Saxon objects demand direct, unmediated encounters. If such encounters are, in fact, made difficult by the uniqueness of these artefacts, their often-distant and secure physical locations, and so on, we nevertheless have a responsibility to at least imagine such direct encounters, even if (or, especially because) such imaginings demand that we step outside the ideology of our most familiar reading practice. And while I cannot yet picture all the results of such imaginings, one immediate observation might be to indicate that textual objects like *Beowulf* and *The Dream of the Rood* may well have only ever had limited distribution in Anglo-Saxon England: rather than reading such works as reflecting the full range of Anglo-Saxon chronology, geography, and culture, we must work even harder to place these objects (and possibly even their antecedent objects) into their proper contexts in place and time. My efforts to historicize the workings of textual production and reproduction demand even greater efforts to historicize the works and poems we read from every period. To refuse the challenges of historicization means to treat these works as texts in our sense, copied, published, and culturally widespread. Of course it remains appropriate to edit these works (in whatever medium) and thus to remake them into the image of our own textuality: but our response to them cannot treat them only as texts in our sense. We must also understand Anglo-Saxon textual artefacts on their own terms, no matter how foreign those terms may seem. Indeed, the very alterity of Anglo-Saxon textual practice is the clearest reason why we must take care to understand it.

The same claim is true, of course, for what I have called Gothic textual practice, in which textual reproduction becomes the ideological norm. But the Gothic period's reliance upon a conception of reproduction as dependent upon a 'moving target' original represents, again, a radical departure from our most familiar ideology of textual reproduction. What understanding the moving target original allows us to do is to properly value textual *variance*, at every level. Where our conventional (print-defined) method of valuing *variance* urges us to imagine an original authorized by the author's hand, a Gothic point of view acknowledges no such controlling original, or at least it acknowledges that no such original can control the form and content of copies, even in an ideological sense. In the Gothic period, the failure inherent in the logic of copying therefore became an active element of textual play, thematized in the classic Gothic literary genres of translation and dream vision, and utilized by both authors and scribes in various sorts of play with aspects of textual definition: paratexts, textual boundaries, images, and the like. This sort of play, it bears reiterating, was literally authorized by the ideology of the 'moving target' original. In a sense, even attempting to copy a manuscript of *The Tales of Caunterbury* without incorporating some aspect of *variance* would have run against the very grain of Gothic textuality: it was not only a practical impossibility, but an ideological one as well.

The consequence of this understanding of Gothic textuality, of course, is to urge us to recognize that there is no such thing as *Piers Plowman* or *The Canterbury Tales*. Rather, there are many *Piers Plowman*s and many *Canterbury Tales*. Our habit of reading these works as if there is such a thing as an authoritative authorial text clearly serves our own ends, and while I remain committed to believing that those ends continue to have a value, we must also take much more seriously the testimony of manuscripts that have been conventionally devalued because they show the highest degree of *variance*. Such manuscripts are not mere corrupt curiosities, but rather exceptional exemplifications of the very underlying textual and media ideology that allowed their reproduction. They surely do not deserve our scorn and lack of attention because they fail to match *our* expectations of what a copy should be. And there is every reason to think that even Chaucer would have celebrated the contributions of Lydgate and the Beryn-poet to *The Tales*. If so, of course, it seems plain that we should do no less.

And when print comes on the scene, the ideology shifts yet again, and not only is it possible to imagine the existence of a perfect, ideal, original, often associated with the author's hand and standing as the object which print seeks to reproduce, it becomes virtually mandatory to imagine such a thing. Here, the technology of typographic print, with its implicit promise of uniformity and identical reproduction of linguistic material, seems to have combined with the logic of copying to result in the new paradigm. That this paradigm is the one that has dominated our culture at least until the present day does nothing to minimize the degree to which it remains a historically localized ideology, even if theorists of language, media, and textuality have sometimes taken it as definitive. The very fact that it is ours, in fact, is the most important reason to make the effort to see beyond it.

As I have discussed it here the central literary form that most clearly expresses the textual ideology of typographic print is the edition, a form which is explicitly dependent upon a split or difference between text and paratext, in which the paratexts serve to define the text and to articulate it as a locus of authority and value. That the text's authority and value needs to be articulated derives from the way print articulates the logic of the copy: printed copies are always understood as failures at representing an ideal text, and thus paratexts must be mobilized to counter that failure. In previous periods, as I argued in Chapters 1 and 2, paratexts served to place a work into the realm of reproduction rather than production, and we see here one exemplification of the ways that the forms of books and literary works often show continuities, despite the important differences in the purposes and effects of those forms in various periods and domains.

But it remains important to note that not all printed books are thoroughly typographic. Whether we consider facsimiles, woodcuts, engravings, or comics, the incorporation of two-dimensional structures of meaning into books and works of literature has always invoked an alternative ideological formation to that demanded by typographic print. Since such two-dimensional structures can never be wholly reduced to linear language, these structures cannot be subject to a controlling ideal, underlying linguistic form. I have called such structures comics, or comics-like, primarily because comics remains the field in which such two-dimensional structures of meaning are put to their clearest literary uses. But also, comics artists in recent decades have most clearly begun exploring the ideological implications of the ways in which comics works escape or refuse both the ideology of typographic print and the structure of the edition.

Specifically, my consideration of long-form comics works by Milt Gross, Art Spiegelman, and Chris Ware suggested that comics works irresistibly pull structures that otherwise appear to be paratexts into the body of the text itself, because of the way in which comics works are productions-in-reproduction. Since comics works cannot reproduce an ideal original, their original printings become the only relevant originals, and when those originals include seeming-paratexts, it often becomes impossible to identify any clear division or separation that can be used to maintain a text/paratext split. And thus when comics works are reprinted, they often become brand new productions, differing perhaps only in small ways from related earlier productions, but ideologically distinct and certainly not mere reproductions of them. Like many produced Anglo-Saxon manuscripts, comics are productions, self-identical originals; like many Gothic literary works, comics often playfully integrate paratextual material right into the text. Likewise, the essential materiality of comics reminds us of the material history of both earlier manuscript periods, as well as suggesting the ways in which the materiality of printed works invokes a comics-style mode of meaning-making. In all of these areas, comics works also allow us to see more clearly how textual (and paratextual) features and structures take on different values and meanings in different ideological domains.

We live at an exciting moment in the history of textual technologies and ideologies, as digital textuality evolves with startling rapidity, seemingly before our very eyes, although perhaps 'hidden in the depths of our reading machines' might be more accurate. What this little book attempts to do is merely to help us understand where we are, and where we have come from, in terms of our ever-evolving textual ideologies. And while my attempt to make a textual gesture of closure and completion (here in this printed book which is an edition, here in this Epilogue, and here in this paragraph) may reveal only how fully I remain engaged in the print paradigm, I also hope this book helps clarify how this very sort of gesture works within the ideology of print that structures my own book's form and its content.

BIBLIOGRAPHY

Manuscript references

Aberystwyth, National Library of Wales, Peniarth 392 D.
Cambridge, Cambridge University Library, KK. 5. 16.
Cambridge, Corpus Christi College, 422.
Dublin, Trinity College Library, A. 4. 5. (57).
Dublin, Trinity College Library, A. 1. (58).
Florence, Bibl. Medicea-Laurenziana, MS Amiatino 1.
Kassel, Landesbibliothek 4° MS. theol. 2.
London, British Library, Cotton Nero D. iv.
London, British Library, Cotton Vespasian B. xiv.
London, British Library, Cotton Vitellius A. xv.
London, British Library, Harley 978.
Northumberland MS 455.
Oxford, Bodleian Library, Hatton 20.
Oxford, Christ Church College 152.
Paris, Bibliothèque nationale, nouv. acq. fr. 1104.
Paris, Bibliothèque nationale, fr. 2168.
Saint Petersburg, National Library of Russia, lat. Q. v. I. 18.
San Marino, CA, Huntington Library, Ellesmere 26 C 9.

Primary sources: editions and facsimiles

Arngart, O., ed., *The Leningrad Bede*, EEMF 2 (Copenhagen: Rosenkilde and Bagger, 1952).
Bately, Janet, ed., *The Old English Orosius*, EETS s.s. 6 (Oxford: EETS, 1980).
Benson, Larry D., ed., *The Riverside Chaucer*, 3rd edition (Boston: Houghton Mifflin, 1987).
Blair, Peter Hunter, ed., *The Moore Bede*, EEMF 9 (Copenhagen: Rosenkilde and Bagger, 1959).
Bowers, John M., ed., *The Canterbury Tales: Fifteenth-Century Continuations and Additions* (Kalamazoo, MI: Medieval Institute Publications, 1992).
Brewer, Charlotte, and A. G. Rigg, *Piers Plowman: A Facsimile of the Z-Text in Bodleian Library Oxford, MS Bodley 851* (Cambridge: D. S. Brewer, 1994).

Bruna, Denis, *Enseignes de Pèlerinage et Enseignes Profanes* (Paris: Éditions de la Réunion des musées nationaux, 1996).

Carnicelli, Thomas A., ed., *King Alfred's Version of St. Augustine's Soliloquies* (Cambridge, MA: Harvard University Press, 1969).

Chaucer, Geoffrey, [*The Canterbury Tales*] ([Westminster: William Caxton, 1477]) [STC 5082, cited via EEBO].

—— [*The Canterbury Tales*] ([Westminster: William Caxton, 1483]) [STC 5083, cited via EEBO].

Colgrave, Bertram, and R. A. B. Mynors, eds. and trans., *Bede's Ecclesiastical History of the English People* (Oxford: Clarendon Press, 1969).

Crotch, W. J. B, ed., *The Prologues and Epilogues of William Caxton*, EETS o.s. 176 (London: EETS, 1928).

Danielewski, Mark, *House of Leaves* (New York: Pantheon, 2000).

Doane, A. N., *The Saxon Genesis* (Madison: University of Wisconsin Press, 1991).

The Ellesmere Manuscript of Chaucer's Canterbury Tales: A Working Facsimile, Introduction by Ralph Hanna III (Cambridge: D. S. Brewer, 1989).

Emerton, Ephraim, trans., *The Letters of Saint Boniface*, with a new introduction and bibliography by Thomas F. X. Noble (New York: Columbia University Press, 2000).

Faletra, Michael A., ed. and trans., *Geoffrey of Monmouth: The History of the Kings of Britain* (Broadview: Peterborough, ON, 2008).

Flower, Robin, and Hugh Smith, *The Parker Chronicle and Laws*, EETS o.s. 208 (Oxford: EETS, 1941 for 1937).

Folsom, Ed, and Kenneth M. Price, eds., *The Walt Whitman Archive* (Lincoln: Center for Digital Research in the Humanities, 1995–2012) <http://www.whitmanarchive.org/>.

Gross, Milt, *He Done Her Wrong: The Great American Novel and Not a Word In It—No Music, Too* (Garden City, NY: Doubleday, Doran & Company, 1930).

—— *He Done Her Wrong: The Great American Novel* (Seattle: Fantagraphics, 2005).

Hinman, Charlton, ed., *The First Folio of Shakespeare: The Norton Facsimile* (New York: W. W. Norton, 1968).

Kane, George, ed., *Piers Plowman: The A Version* (London: Athlone Press, 1960).

—— and E. Talbot Donaldson, eds., *Piers Plowman: The B Version* (London: Athlone Press, 1975).

Krapp, George Philip, and Elliott V. K. Dobbie, eds., *The Anglo-Saxon Poetic Records*, 6 vols. (New York: Columbia University Press, 1931–53).

Lowe, E. A., ed., *Codices Latini Antiquiores*, Supplement (Oxford: Clarendon Press, 1971).

—— *Codices Latini Antiquiores*, vol. II [Great Britain and Ireland] (Oxford: Clarendon Press, 1972).

Meech, Sanford Brown, ed., *The Book of Margery Kempe*, EETS o.s. 212, with prefatory note and appendices by Hope Emily Allen (Oxford: EETS, 1940).

Moore, Alan (writer) and Dave Gibbons (artist), *Watchmen* (New York: DC Comics, 1987), 3rd printing.

More, Sir Thomas, *Utopia: A New Translation*, Norton Critical Edition, trans. and ed. Robert M. Adams (New York: Norton, 1975).

Parker, Matthew, *A Testimonie of Antiquitie* (London: John Day, 1566).

Pynchon, Thomas, *V.* (Philadelphia: Lippincott, 1963).

Ruggiers, Paul G., ed., *The Canterbury Tales: A Facsimile and Transcription of the Hengwrt Manuscript, with Variants from the Hengwrt Manuscript* (Norman, OK: University of Oklahoma Press, 1979).

Russell, George, and George Kane, eds., *Piers Plowman: The C Version* (London: Athlone Press, 1997).

Rychner, Jean, ed., *Les Lais de Marie de France* (Paris: Éditions Champion, 1969).

Scragg, Donald, ed., *The Vercelli Homilies*, EETS o.s. 300 (Oxford: EETS, 1992).

Shakespeare, William, *Mr. William Shakespeares Comedies, Histories, & Tragedies* (London: Isaac Iaggard and Ed. Blount, 1623) [STC 22273].

—— *Mr. William Shakespeares Comedies, Histories, & Tragedies* (London: Robert Allot, 1632) [STC 22274].

—— *Mr. William Shakespear's Comedies, Histories, & Tragedies* (London: P. C., 1664) [Wing S2914].

—— *Mr. William Shakespear's Comedies, Histories, & Tragedies* (London: H. Herringman, E. Brewster, and R. Bentley, 1985) [Wing S2915].

Skeat, W. W., ed., *The Vision of William Concerning Piers the Plowman in Three Parallel Texts* (Oxford: Oxford University Press, 1886).

Spencer, Brian, *Pilgrim Souvenirs and Secular Badges: Medieval Finds from Excavations in London* (London: The Stationery Office, 1998).

Spiegelman, Art, *Maus: A Survivor's Tale* (New York: Pantheon, 1986).

—— *Maus A Survivor's Tale I: My Father Bleeds History* (New York: Pantheon, 1986 [*recte* 1991]).

—— *Maus A Survivor's Tale II: And Here My Troubles Began* (New York: Pantheon, 1991).

—— *In the Shadow of No Towers* (New York: Pantheon, 2004).

Swanton, Michael, ed., *The Dream of the Rood*, new edition (Exeter: University of Exeter Press, 1996).

Tangl, Michael, ed., *Die Briefe des Heilegen Bonifatius und Lullus*, 2nd edition (Berlin: Weidmannische Verlagsbuchhandlung, 1955).

Tolkien, J. R. R., *The Lord of the Rings* (Boston: Houghton Mifflin, 2004).

van Beuningen, H. J. E., and A. M. Koldeweij, *Heilig en Profaan: 1000 Laatmiddeleeuwse Insignes uit de Collectie H. J. E. van Beuningen*, Rotterdam Papers VIII (Cothen: Stichting Middeleeuwse Religieuze en Profane Insignes, 1993).

—— —— and D. Kicken, *Heilig en Profaan 2: 1200 Laatmiddeleeuwse Insignes uit Openbare en Particuliere Collecties*, Rotterdam Papers XII (Cothen: Stichting Middeleeuwse Religieuze en Profane Insignes, 2001).

Ware, Chris, *Jimmy Corrigan: The Smartest Kid on Earth* (New York: Pantheon, 2000), 3rd printing.

—— *Jimmy Corrigan: The Smartest Kid on Earth* (New York: Pantheon, 2003), 4th paperback printing.

—— *The Acme Novelty Library Final Report to Shareholders* (New York: Pantheon, 2005).

Ware, F. C., *Quimby the Mouse* (Seattle: Fantagraphics, 2003).

Wilcox, Jonathan, ed., *Ælfric's Prefaces* (Durham: Durham Medieval Texts, 1994).

Zettersten, Arne, ed., *Waldere* (Manchester: Manchester University Press, 1979).

Zupitza, Julius, *Beowulf Reproduced in Facsimile*, EETS o.s. 77 (London: EETS, 1882).

—— *Beowulf Reproduced in Facsimile*, 2nd edition, with an Introductory Note by Norman Davis, EETS o.s. 245 (London: Oxford University Press, 1959).

Secondary sources

Abel, Jessica, and Matt Madden, 'Foreword', in Alison Bechdel, ed., *The Best American Comics 2011* (Boston: Houghton Mifflin, 2011), pp. vii–xii.

Abels, Richard, 'What Has Weland to Do with Christ? The Franks Casket and the Acculturation of Christianity in Early Anglo-Saxon England', *Speculum* 84 (2009), 549–81.

Anderson, Douglas A., 'Note on the Text', in J. R. R. Tolkien, *The Lord of the Rings* (Boston: Houghton Mifflin, 2004), pp. xi–xvii.

Baudrillard, Jean, *Simulations*, trans. Paul Foss, Paul Patton, and Philip Beitchman (New York: Semiotext(e), 1983).

Benson, C. David, *Public Piers Plowman: Modern Scholarship and Late Medieval English Culture* (Philadelphia: University of Pennsylvania Press, 2004).

Bolter, Jay David, and Richard Grusin, *Remediation: Understanding New Media* (Cambridge, MA: MIT Press, 1999).

Bredehoft, Thomas A., *Textual Histories: Readings in the Anglo-Saxon Chronicle* (Toronto: University of Toronto Press, 2001).

—— *Early English Metre* (Toronto: University of Toronto Press, 2005).

—— 'Comics Architecture, Multidimensionality, and Time: Chris Ware's *Jimmy Corrigan: The Smartest Kid on Earth*', *Mfs* 52.4 (2006), 869–90.

—— 'Literacy without Letters: Pilgrim Badges and Late-Medieval Literate Ideology', *Viator* 37 (2006), 433–45.

—— *Authors, Audiences, and Old English Verse* (Toronto: University of Toronto Press, 2009).

—— 'The Gothic Turn in Twelfth-Century English Chronicles', in Elaine Treharne and Greg Walker, eds., *The Oxford Handbook of Medieval Literature in English* (Oxford: Oxford University Press, 2010), pp. 353–69.

—— 'Style, Voice, and Authorship in Harvey Pekar's (Auto)(Bio)Graphical Comics', *College Literature* 38.3 (2011), 97–110.

—— 'Three New Cryptic Runes on the Franks Casket', *Notes and Queries* N.S. 58.2 (2011), 181–3.

Brooks, Nicholas, *The Early History of the Church of Canterbury* (London: Leicester University Press, 1996).

Brown, Michelle P., 'The Triumph of the Codex: The Manuscript Book Before 1100', in Simon Eliot and Jonathan Rose, eds., *A Companion to the History of the Book* (Oxford: Blackwell, 2007), pp. 179–93.

Cates, Isaac, 'Comics and the Grammar of Diagrams', in David M. Ball and Martha B. Kuhlman, eds., *The Comics of Chris Ware: Drawing is a Way of Thinking* (Jackson, MS: University Press of Mississippi, 2010), pp. 90–104.

Cave, Terence, ed., *Thomas More's* Utopia *in Early Modern Europe: Paratexts and Contexts* (Manchester: Manchester University Press, 2008).

Cerquiglini, Bernard, *In Praise of the Variant: A Critical History of Philology*, trans. Betsy Wing (Baltimore: Johns Hopkins University Press, 1999).

Derolez, Albert, *The Palaeography of Gothic Manuscript Books from the Twelfth to the Early Sixteenth Century* (Cambridge: Cambridge University Press, 2003).

Derrida, Jacques, 'Plato's Pharmacy', in *Dissemination*, trans. Barbara Johnson (Chicago: University of Chicago Press, 1981), pp. 61–171.

Donoghue, Daniel, *Style in Old English Poetry: The Test of the Auxiliary* (New Haven: Yale University Press, 1987).

Echard, Siân, *Printing the Middle Ages* (Philadelphia: University of Pennsylvania Press, 2008).

Edwards, A. S. G., 'The Ellesmere Manuscript: Controversy, Culture, and the *Canterbury Tales*', in Orietta Da Rold and Elaine Treharne, eds., *Textual Cultures: Cultural Texts* (Cambridge: D. S. Brewer, 2010), pp. 59–73.

Folsom, Ed, *Whitman Making Books, Books Making Whitman* (Iowa City: The Obermann Center for Advanced Studies, 2005).

Foucault, Michel, 'What is an Author?', in Paul Rabinow, ed., *The Foucault Reader* (New York: Pantheon, 1984), pp. 101–20.

Fuhrmann, Otto W., *Gutenberg and the Strasbourg Documents of 1439: An Inter-pretation* (New York: Press of the Woolly Whale, 1940).

Genette, Gérard, *Paratexts: Thresholds of Interpretation*, trans. Jane E. Lewin (Cambridge: Cambridge University Press, 1987).

Gillespie, Alexandra, *Print Culture and the Medieval Author: Chaucer, Lydgate, and Their Books 1473–1557* (Oxford: Oxford University Press, 2006).

Hanna III, Ralph, *William Langland*. Authors of the Middle Ages 3 (Aldershot: Variorum, 1993).

Harvey, Robert C., 'Comedy at the Juncture of Word and Image', in Robin Varnum and Christina T. Gibbons, eds., *The Language of Comics: Word and Image* (Jackson, MS: University Press of Mississippi, 2001), pp. 75–96.

Hathaway, Rosemary, 'Reading Art Spiegelman's *Maus* as Postmodern Ethnography', *Journal of Folklore Research* 48.3 (2011), 249–67.

Heer, Jeet, 'Inventing Cartooning Ancestors: Ware and the Comics Canon', in David M. Ball and Martha B. Kuhlman, eds., *The Comics of Chris Ware: Drawing is a Way of Thinking* (Jackson, MS: University Press of Mississippi, 2010), pp. 3–13.

Kannenberg, Gene, 'The Comics of Chris Ware: Text, Image, and Visual Narrative Strategies', in Robin Varnum and Christina T. Gibbons, eds., *The Language of Comics: Word and Image* (Jackson, MS: University Press of Mississippi, 2001), pp. 174–97.

Ker, N. R., *A Catalogue of Manuscripts Containing Anglo-Saxon* (Oxford: Clarendon Press, 1957).

Kiernan, Kevin, *Beowulf and the Beowulf Manuscript*, revised edition (Ann Arbor: University of Michigan Press, 1996).

Kuskin, William, *Symbolic Caxton: Literary Culture and Print Capitalism* (Notre Dame, IN: University of Notre Dame Press, 2008).

Lapidge, Michael, 'The Archetype of *Beowulf*', *Anglo-Saxon England* 29 (2000), 5–41.

McCloud, Scott, *Understanding Comics: The Invisible Art* (New York: Harper-Perennial, 1994).

Mitchell, Bruce, and Fred C. Robinson, *A Guide to Old English*, 7th edition (Oxford: Blackwell, 2007).

Mooney, Linne R., 'Chaucer's Scribe', *Speculum* 86 (2006), 97–138.

Napier, Arthur, 'Contributions to Old English Literature: 1. An Old English Homily on the Observance of Sunday. 2. The Franks Casket', in W. P. Ker, A. S. Napier, and W. W. Skeat, eds., *An English Miscellany presented to Dr. F. J. Furnivall* (reprint edn. New York: AMS, 1969), pp. 355–81.

Pasternack, Carol Braun, *The Textuality of Old English Poetry*. Cambridge Studies in Anglo-Saxon England 13 (Cambridge: Cambridge University Press, 1995).

Raeburn, Daniel, 'Building a Language', in Daniel Raeburn, *Chris Ware* (New Haven: Yale University Press, 2004), pp. 6–26.

Roberts, Jane, '*The Finnsburh Fragment*, and its Lambeth Provenance', *Notes and Queries* N.S. 55.2 (2008), 122–4.

Robinson, Fred C., 'Old English Literature in its Most Immediate Context', in John D. Niles, ed., *Old English Literature in Context* (Cambridge: D. S. Brewer, 1980), pp. 11–29.

Smith, Margaret M., *The Title Page: Its Early Development, 1460–1510* (London and New Castle, DE: The British Library and Oak Knoll Press, 2000).

—— 'Red as a Textual Element during the Transition from Manuscript to Print', in Orietta Da Rold and Elaine Treharne, eds., *Textual Cultures: Cultural Texts* (Cambridge: D. S. Brewer, 2010), pp. 187–200.

Spiegelman, Art, *MetaMaus* (New York: Pantheon 2011).

Tanselle, G. Thomas, *A Rationale of Textual Criticism* (Philadelphia: University of Pennsylvania Press, 1989).

Treharne, Elaine, 'The Architextual Editing of Early English', *Poetica* 71 (2009), 1–13.

Vandendorpe, Christian, *From Papyrus to Hypertext: Towards the Universal Digital Library* (Urbana: University of Illinois Press, 2009).

Warner, Lawrence, *The Lost History of* Piers Plowman (Philadelphia: University of Pennsylvania Press, 2011).

INDEX